P9-BYE-221

This book belongs in every home in this country, military or not. The stories are so well-written that I could almost smell the jet fuel, hear the gunfire, and taste the joy of freedom.

ELLIE KAY
AUTHOR AND USAF SPOUSE

This book affirms that you can be a warrior and a Christian; and if you are both, the military unit you serve will be better off because of it. The stories of Christian military men and women carrying out their duties, guided by their deep faith in Christ, rings true to my experiences. It also characterizes the best commanders I've served under during my 31 years in the infantry. *Taking the High Ground* is a great book, and I recommend it especially to those who some day might be called upon to make tough decisions.

GILES F. CRIDER ★ COLONEL, U.S. ARMY (RET.)
EXECUTIVE DIRECTOR, MILITARY MINISTRY
CAMPUS CRUSADE FOR CHRIST

Jeff O'Leary gets to the heart of what it means to be in the service of God and country: death and birth, captivity and freedom, suffering and forgiveness, separation and togetherness, war and peace, defeat and victory.

BRUCE L. FISTER ★ LIEUTENANT GENERAL, USAF (RET.)
EXECUTIVE DIRECTOR,
OFFICERS' CHRISTIAN FELLOWSHIP

Jeff O'Leary introduces us to ordinary people in extraordinary circumstances—people who have found faith, courage, determination, fortitude, and love in the course of carrying out their duties. Take the high ground by reading this book!

DICK ABEL ★ BRIG. GENERAL, USAF (RET.)
EXECUTIVE DIRECTOR, MILITARY MINISTRY
CAMPUS CRUSADE FOR CHRIST

★   ★   ★

Colonel O'Leary is also a sought-after speaker. His life, military service, leadership, and contact with a variety of cultures provide him with a unique ability to offer highly motivational presentations.

TAKING THE HIGH GROUND

MILITARY MOMENTS WITH GOD

COLONEL JEFFREY O'LEARY

Run So That You May Win

ivictor.com

Victor is an imprint of
Cook Communications Ministries, Colorado Springs, Colorado 80918
Cook Communications, Paris, Ontario
Kingsway Communications, Eastbourne, England

TAKING THE HIGH GROUND
© 2001 by Jeffrey O'Leary

All rights reserved. No part of this book may be reproduced without
written permission, except for brief quotations in books and critical
reviews. For information, write Cook Communications Ministries, 4050 Lee
Vance View, Colorado Springs, Colorado 80918.

First Printing, 2001
Printed in the United States of America

1 2 3 4 5 6 7 8 9 10 Printing/Year 05 04 03 02 01

Editor: Lee Hough
Cover and Interior Design: Design Concepts

Unless otherwise noted, Scripture quotations are taken from *The New
King James Version.* © 1979, 1980, 1982, Thomas Nelson, Inc., Publishers.
Other Scripture quotations taken from the *Holy Bible: New International
Version*® (NIV). Copyright © 1973, 1978, 1984 by International Bible Society.
Used by permission of Zondervan Publishing House. All rights reserved;
New American Standard Bible (NASB), © the Lockman Foundation 1960,
1962, 1963, 1968, 1971, 1972, 1973, 1975, 1977; The *Holy Bible*, New Living
Translation (NLT), © 1966. Used by permission of Tyndale House Publishers,
Inc., Wheaton, Illinois 60189; *Revised Standard Version of the Bible* (RSV), ©
1946, 1952, 1971, 1973; and *Authorized (King James) Version* (KJV).

Library of Congress Cataloging-in-Publication Data

O'Leary, Jeffrey.
        Taking the high ground : military moments with God / Jeffrey
O'Leary.
        p. cm.
        ISBN 0-7814-3541-2
        1. Armed forces—Prayer-books and devotions—English. I. Title.

BV4588 .O54 2001
242'.68—dc21
                                        00-054547

To my best friend, my breath, my wife,
Cindy

Colonel Jeff O'Leary can be reached at www.jeffoleary.com for speaking engagements. Information about Mission of Joy and its work among orphans can be found at www.missionjoy.org.

Share Your Stories with Us

Presently, we are in the process of putting together a series of books like these, including a second edition of this book: Taking the High Ground—*More* Military Moments with God. Whether you're a mom or dad, single or married, young or old, we're interested in reading <u>your</u> inspirational story.

If you have stories that are uplifting, humorous, encouraging, thought-provoking or heart-rending, we invite you to send them to us for publication.

Information on submitting your story can be found at our web site or by e-mailing us. You may also submit your stories by mail to:

Jeffrey O'Leary
Military Moments with God
PO Box 6591
Woodbridge, VA 22195

If you found this book particularly meaningful, we would love to hear from you. Tell us about how this book touched your life—we will use some of your letters in the next book.

CONTENTS

★

A C K N O W L E D G E M E N T S

WHEN LEE HOUGH, THEN PRODUCT MANAGER FOR COOK COMMUNICATIONS, ASKED ME IF I WOULD BE INTERESTED IN WRITING THIS BOOK, I PUSHED BACK. Working in the Pentagon, managing a nonprofit ministry for orphans, and raising five children of my own kept me *more* than busy. Further, I didn't have the faintest idea who Cook was.

"Lee," I said, "as far as I know, you could be calling me from a garage where you print your books." To his enormous credit, he took my comment in stride, laughed, and invited me for a visit.

I took him up on his offer and discovered that Cook was not only a significant publisher, but shared my heart for missions. So I couldn't help but agree to the book you now hold.

I want to thank the editorial staff at Cook—Craig Bubeck, Julie Smith, and Alice Crider—for providing excellent, though often painful, editorial feedback.

I am also grateful for the professional advice I've received from fellow author Ellie Kay. You passed the wisdom learned from your first book *Shop, Save and Share,* and I profited immensely. Thanks also, to Leisha Joseph who recommended that Cook take a look at this unknown writer to pen this book. Since his, recent move to Alive Communications, Lee Hough has helped me enormously as my agent. Thank you, Lee! Your friendship means as much as your professional guidance.

Two organizations that helped me gather material and recommended individual contributors for the book: Campus Crusade for

Christ Military Ministries and Officer's Christian Fellowship. Your partnership was exemplary of the brotherhood of fellowship we all share in Christ.

To my mother, Miriam O'Leary, who put her years of teaching experience to great use. Along with a multitude of grammar corrections, she provided insightful editing to ensure even non-military types could appreciate the book.

Finally, I'd like to remember my family for enduring this year in which they spent less time with me than they were entitled. Thank you for your patience and encouragement along the way: Cindy, my wife, and my children: Jo Beth, Stephen, Kjerstin, Sean, and Shannon. I love you all.

Finally Lord, I lay this pen at Your feet. I pray You will be glorified and uplifted through the words that follow. Open the eyes of the blind that they may see how very much You love them. Be glorified, alone and forever.

★

HOW DO WE PASS ON OUR GREATEST TREASURES TO THOSE WHO COME AFTER US? If we value things, then passing them on involves matters of the law. But when it comes to matters of the heart, character, and conscience, the method seems more uncertain. Whether these matters of the heart are called Christian virtues, family values, or military traditions, the challenge remains. We must press with all our strength to leave footprints deep enough to serve as timeless markers along the way. I believe this task is more important than ever as a culture once sure and swift now wanders and drifts.

The day comes when we must pass the torch of leadership to new leaders and new believers. We are given a brief moment to acquaint those behind us with the strength and blessing of the heritage we've received. Our faith and demonstration of living virtue will be the standards by which our words will be judged hollow or ring true.

In the pages that follow are stories of military men and women who served not only their nation, but also God, honorably and with courage. It has been a truly humbling experience to have so many share their most significant moments with me. I feel a special trust to faithfully carry these stories to you. Most of these were gathered via interviews, some as written recollections, but all leave behind indelible footprints. The contributor's names are given with their stories. Those without an author named are my stories.

These footprints can be followed, for they are not fables or fantasies, but the gritty reality of Christian faith in a harsh world. It is upon the high seas, in the muddy trenches, and in the fighter cockpit that we find Christ is able to be all He has promised.

These treasures were given to me, and now I give them to you. They are treasures contained in earthen vessels. Be prepared: you are dealing with vessels of clay. As such, you will see imperfections along the way. But these clay vessels, of which I am one, have found God more than sufficient to overcome our own weaknesses. May He be your strength, as He has proven to be ours.

With that, I lay down my pen and pray:

> How shall broken hands
> Craft means by which
> Men shall see and praise You?
> "It cannot be done," whispers my weakness
> "Pretender!" cries my accuser
> I bow my head and raise my broken hands,
> "It is true, my hands are broken," I reply.
> Yet, yet
> "Oh Lord, You can make my weakness strength
> If You will,
> Make this foolish thing wise and
> Bring praise to Your throne, once more—
> Through these broken hands."

Jeffrey O'Leary

To everything there is a season,
A time for every purpose under heaven

Ecclesiastes 3:1

A Time for Every Season

Spring still makes spring in the mind
When sixty years are told:
Love wakes anew this throbbing heart,
And we are never old.
Over the winter glaciers
I see the summer glow,
And through the wild-piled snowdrift
The warm rosebuds below.

Ralph Waldo Emerson

I purpose to fight it out on this line
if it takes all summer.
If you see the President,
tell him that whatever happens
there will be no turning back.

Ulysses S. Grant, May 1864

FALL AWAKENING:
FIREFIGHT IN THE MEKONG

★

JIM MUKOYAMA
MAJOR GENERAL, US ARMY (RETIRED)

"You have heard that it was said, 'You shall love your neighbor and hate your enemy.' But I say to you, love your enemies, bless those who curse you, do good to those who hate you, and pray for those who spitefully use you and persecute you, that you may be sons of your Father in heaven" (Matt. 5: 43-45).

The chopper blades beat the air with a familiar "whup whup whup" sound as I climbed into the back of the green camouflaged Huey. The door gunner swiveled the M-60 and checked the safety as the rotor blades began to spin faster as the pilots throttled down. The skids of our half-hovering chopper shifted from side to side and then, with one final thrust of power, the Huey nosed forward and pitched up. We were off on another mission.

I had been "in-country" about three months and this was my sixth such outing. As a company commander, I had 120 men under my command for this operation. The number of available transportation helicopters, or "slicks," limited the number of troops I could bring. I would lead this reconnaissance in force mission for the next two to three days in the jungle, canals, and rice paddies of the Delta. Our mission was to make contact with the VC, find out what we could, and eliminate any hostile elements we ran into.

I was like many other army captains in Vietnam. We were all trying to get the job done without screwing it up. We were focused on our job and our men and were too busy to reflect on everything else that was going on.

I had come to know the Lord at a Moody Bible Institute camp when I was a preteen and had remained active in my youth group throughout high school. During my years in college and Army ROTC,

I continued to be an active believer.

Looking back, though, I could see how the elements of violence and war had jaded my views. I had spent a previous thirteen-month tour in the Korean DMZ where we had twelve soldiers killed and forty wounded in my battalion. After a short trip stateside, the army selected me to command an Air Mobile Company of the Ninth Division, in the Mekong Delta region of Vietnam.

The humidity and heat seemed to dissipate as we cruised above the jungle's multi-green shades. Coming in low, we crossed a variety of canals and rice paddies so common along the Delta. I looked at the men in the chopper with me. Their eyes were fixed and their hands tightly gripped their weapons. It was always tense before we descended to the LZ (landing zone), and today would be no different.

The pilot dropped the chopper like a rock to the LZ and the door-gunners opened up with their M-60s along the tree line. Yelling "Go! Go! Go!" I jumped to the ground and our company fanned out establishing a 360-degree zone of security. I established radio contact with all my platoon leaders and we cautiously advanced toward the tree line.

Initially, we crossed a series of rice paddies and then moved into the surrounding jungle. It was to be a three-day mission, but within a few hours we heard the deadly popcorn sound of small arms fire erupting around us.

My company opened fire and aggressively pursued the enemy. It appeared to be a small unit of VC, and we had surprised them. Approaching a small village from three sides, we bracketed them in and carefully closed the ground between us and their gunfire. Then, almost as suddenly as it had begun, the return fire ceased. Weapons at the ready, my company methodically checked and cleared each hut and building in the village.

I entered the village to find three dead VC lying near each other. I picked up the radio and, with the adrenaline still pumping, I began to give orders to my platoon leaders.

I knew the most vulnerable time for a unit in combat was just after a successful firefight. It was human nature to let one's guard down and breathe a sigh of relief—just the time for an enemy counterattack. It was my responsibility to kick "rear end" and get everyone's attention to reorganize, redistribute ammo, look for likely enemy avenues of approach, and take care of the wounded.

I handed over the radio and looked down at my feet. Three dead VC, and we had survived without a scratch. I took a deep breath in relief and began to walk away. I had a hundred men to see to. I started to bark out more orders, but looked back again at the dead VC lying on the ground. Suddenly I felt very uncomfortable.

Then it hit me. I stopped in my tracks and looked back at those men lying dead in the dirt. It was like an arrow shot into my heart. What had happened to my humanity? How was it I felt nothing for these men? I was overcome with a sense of regret that I didn't share with the men around me. I believed in God and had trusted Christ with my life. Surely that should mean I would be different. But I was becoming numb to the violence and death around me. I had to do something to change that. Whether I changed anyone else hardly mattered. I needed to change.

So I stood over those dead Viet Cong and prayed for them. They had families, and they had loved their wives and children. They had loved their country enough to fight against those they considered their enemies. And then I prayed for myself. In the end, I think my prayers were as much for me as they were for them. I didn't stop for long, but the entire episode has remained a vivid memory.

I walked away from that battle with a lighter load on my shoulders. It was a victory for our company, yes. But it was a greater victory for me. Through prayer and forgiveness, I had won the battle over my darker nature.

It was Longfellow who echoed my thoughts and the battle I faced that day; not the battle without, but the battle within. It was a lesson I would not soon forget.

"Not in the clamor of the crowded street,
Not in the shouts and plaudits of the throng,
But in ourselves, are triumph and defeat."
Longfellow

WINTER'S SLEEP:
B-52 DOWN

★

Indeed, You have made my days as handbreadths,
And my age is as nothing before You;
Certainly every man at his best state is but vapor (Ps. 39:5).

There was always something special about watching B-52s take-off in MITO formation—Minimum Interval Take-Off—and the interval on that cold day in December was twelve seconds between three fully loaded B-52s. I was not flying that day, so I stood near the alert shack and watched as the three B-52s taxied into position. The black smoke from the first bomber poured out of the exhaust as it released brakes and added water to the eight TF33 turbofan Pratt and Whitney engines, each producing 17,000 pounds of thrust. The effect of a water assisted take-off was significant in helping a 450,000-pound bomber achieve greater power in take-off and initial climb out.

As a second lieutenant, I had watched only a few of these, but as the second jet cleared the ground, I could tell something wasn't right. The plane appeared to have been overtaking the first jet, and as it cleared the ground veered to the right, then back to the left, then back to the right again. By now, the jet was 500 feet beyond the end of the runway and was rapidly banking through thirty degrees to forty degrees; and as it descended, it went into a full ninety degrees of bank. Within five more seconds the plane's right wing touched ground and the rest of the airplane followed in an explosive fireball ignited by 200,000 pounds of jet fuel.

I heard the words from the alert speaker, "B-52 down, B-52 down, B-52 down." Racing from the alert shack to a waiting vehicle, I headed to the crash site near the end of the runway. Flames were visible and the heat and smoke were overwhelming.

With sirens screaming, numerous emergency vehicles soon filled the area. It was then that it hit me: none of the nine crew members had initiated an ejection sequence. Certainly that wasn't surprising for the three instructors who weren't seated in ejection seats. But I wondered *why didn't any of the primary six crew members eject?* As the smoke cleared, and the wreckage became more visible, it was obvious there would be no survivors. I walked away stunned and feeling empty. *I could have been flying that day.*

The next morning the squadron commander called me into his office and asked if I'd be the military escort for one of the officers who had been killed in the crash. It's not the kind of job anyone would ever ask for and the kind of job no one would turn down. It was the least I could do. The military escort helps the family with the funeral arrangements and personally accompanies the casket at all phases of the flight to the final resting place. When the plane touched down, I was the first off the aircraft and made sure the flag covered the casket as I accompanied it to the hearse. Once the body was at the funeral home, I went to the family's home.

The son of this grieving family had been all of twenty-two and was the same rank as I—a second lieutenant. As I explained to the family who I was, they welcomed me into their home. Over the next several days, we spent many hours together.

I didn't know their son and they took great pains to acquaint me with him. There wasn't a lot I could say, so I kept quiet, listened, and stayed close. Through my time with the parents, I learned in such situations there are no satisfying answers. They wondered why their son was dead. I wondered why none of the crew managed to get out. But by being there during the grieving process, I could be a satisfying companion and provide a compassionate listening ear. It was a sobering experience for a young officer with lots of airspeed and less direction.

At the graveside ceremony, three jets flew overhead in missing man formation, the bugler played taps, the honor guard fired its salute, and we moved slowly to the limousine that awaited the family. I said my good-byes and promised to keep in touch as I watched them drive away. Opening my car door, I turned back to look at the black box covered with roses poised over the hole in the ground. I realized that I was very grateful. I was grateful to be alive, certainly. But mostly, I was grateful I had seen life for what it really was; a morning mist too quickly burned off and a brief gift of God, to be honored and treasured. Every moment of it.

SPRING HOPE: FREEDOM ROAD THROUGH CHECKPOINT CHARLIE

★

The Spirit of the Lord is upon Me, Because He has anointed Me to preach the gospel to the poor; He has sent Me to heal the broken-hearted, To proclaim liberty to the captives And recovery of sight to the blind, To set at liberty those who are oppressed (Luke 4:18).

"There is hope in your future," says the Lord, "That your children shall come back to their own border" (Jer. 31:17).

I recently spent a week in Berlin on military business. It had been a decade since the fall of the Soviet Union when I stepped off the airplane at Berlin-Tegel airport. I wondered how much had changed since the wall came down.

As I traveled past the famous Brandenburg gate, I realized I crossed in a moment what had separated millions for almost thirty years. It was the place where American and East German tanks faced off in 1961. It was the place where President Kennedy stood and declared:

> Freedom has many difficulties and democracy is not perfect, but we have never had to put a wall up to keep our people in, to prevent them from leaving us. . . . Freedom is indivisible, and when one man is enslaved, all are not free.

My agent booked me into a hotel in what had been East Berlin.

Across from my hotel was the plaza on Unter den Linden, where the Nazis burned thousands of books in the early 1930s. A bit farther was the building that housed the headquarters of the East German Stasi secret police. Another short walk away stood what was Gestapo Headquarters during Hitler's rule. But what drew me most was the flashpoint between east and west, between democracy and communism, and between freedom and chains. That place was known as Checkpoint Charlie.

Approaching Checkpoint Charlie from the Soviet Sector, I read the sign that warned East Germans, "You are now leaving the Soviet Sector." A photograph of an American soldier was displayed next to it. I walked a little farther into the American sector and turned around. A photograph of a Soviet soldier stared at me next to an ominous sign that warned, "You are now leaving the American sector."

Still remaining at the checkpoint was a control tower where East German border guards had kept watch. On either side of the checkpoint were several buildings whose windows were bricked over to prevent escapes.

This description may seem irrelevant, as looking back, for many, seems a waste of time. For me, having spent many years on B-52 alert, walking in the Soviet Sector was a surreal experience. I had spent half a lifetime ensuring both the safety of Americans and an idea we believed in. We call it freedom.

Many people consider that notion somewhat passé today. Yet Jesus understood the human need to be free. He spoke to a subjugated Jewish people under Roman rule when he promised, "When the Son makes you free, you will be free indeed" (John 8:36). There is a thirst for freedom in the human spirit that is rarely understood or appreciated until it is taken away.

As conditions deteriorated in the East after WWII, more than three million East Germans fled to the West. The Soviet answer to this massive bleeding was to build a wall. Within a period of one month, eighteen million Germans lost the freedom to leave their borders.

During the first week of the east/west standoff, barbed wire was strung across fifteen miles of the border area. A famous picture was snapped as a five-year-old child stood at the fence with his hands outspread—seeking and hoping to be free. A youthful looking East German guard compassionately opens the wire for the child to climb through to freedom. At the same time, the guard is looking to the side to see if his superiors have observed him. The child gained his freedom while the guard, who was observed, was arrested and taken away.

Within one year more than one hundred observation towers were built. Nearly every East German house within two hundred yards of the border was torn down and the occupants forced to move.

Until the buildings were torn down, a stream of freedom seekers jumped from the windows into sheets held by West Germans below. Young babies were thrown from the windows while the very old jumped as well. Soon, bricks began to cover every open window where escapes could occur.

As the barbed wire was replaced by a strong wall, escape attempts became more dangerous and sometimes more violent. Trucks full of people crashed at high speed into the wall. Some managed to run to freedom while snipers in observation towers killed many others. Those who were caught were taken to trial and given lengthy prison sentences.

After five years, fortifications increased to 230 guard towers. Weapons trained to fire automatically at moving targets protected kill zones for hundreds of yards. Land mines were placed throughout the zone. Tank traps were spread side by side for dozens of miles, and various interior walls and barbed wire were strung to stem the flight. Still, the people came.

Tunnels were built across the shortest distances between east and west. Cavities were carved in automobiles, trucks, electrical generators, and furniture to hide people hoping to find freedom. Some famous escapes involved even more ingenious methods. One family of eight managed to build a hot air balloon and escape. Others built small sail planes, hang-gliders, and even a small submerged submarine to escape to freedom. Even those who served as border guards experienced this thirst for freedom. Over twenty-eight years, more than two thousand dropped their weapons and ran to freedom.

Tragedies were regular fare for those shot in the no-man's zone. Caught between East and West, they bled to death under both the passionless and pained eyes of frozen watchers. And occasionally, a shining moment of promise broke through, when guards would rush into the zone of death, risking themselves, to save one.

No description of this length can adequately explain the terror and thirst for freedom that existed in East Germany for nearly thirty years. At best, I can evoke what memories still remain.

I had a chance to bring a piece of the wall home with me. I thought about it but couldn't do it. Too much misery was in that wall. Too many families divided, too many deaths, and too many fellow believers were wounded and killed by that wall. I turned away and boarded my plane.

I left Berlin with a sacred appreciation of the heritage of freedom I'd been given. I also left with a deeper knowledge of the cost Christ paid to take down the wall that separated me from God. The road to freedom has always been through killing zones, from Calvary to Checkpoint Charlie. The price of freedom, then and now, has always been too costly. The currency has always been blood.

SUMMER ESCAPE: COLONEL GEORGE WASHINGTON, BELOVED ENEMY

★

When a man's ways please the Lord,
he makes even his enemies to be at peace with him (Prov. 16:7).

Colonel George Washington joined the Virginia militia in 1753 and received a special commission from the British governor in Virginia. He was sent on a diplomatic mission to the Ohio River valley to expel the French from the region. It was what we would call, in this century, gunboat diplomacy on horseback. He was twenty-one years old.

Serving under General Braddock proved to be an illuminating experience that would serve him well in the Revolutionary War some twenty years later.

On July 9, 1755, Colonel Washington, along with more than eighty officers and over thirteen hundred men, moved slowly toward an area known as Monongahela. Hoping to expel the French from Fort Duquesne, they were within ten miles of their target when they were ambushed. Hidden by trees, French and Indians lined the sides of the ravine above them and boxed them in at both ends of the valley.

The British troops under General Braddock reacted the way armies of Europe did in that day. They stood side by side and returned fire in an orderly prescribed manner. They couldn't run and they couldn't hide. So they did what they could to survive what soon became a slaughter.

In a period of two hours, more than half of Braddock's command was killed or wounded. General Braddock himself was killed and all officers on horseback had been shot from their mounts. Washington himself had two horses shot out from underneath him;

yet he found remounts each time to continue the battle. By the time the engagement ended, he was the only officer left on horseback.

According to Washington's own journal, he took off his jacket following the battle and found four bullet holes through it.[1] Yet, he hadn't even been scratched! Washington gave glory to God for preserving him. He wrote his brother saying, "death was leveling my companions on every side of me, but by the all-powerful dispensations of Providence, I have been protected."[2]

Raised by a strong Christian mother, Washington had been taught the priority of prayer, which he took to heart. The prayer journal he kept, with both notes and prayers filling it, demonstrated he was well acquainted with the Lord in the privacy of his prayer closet.

Some fifteen years later, Washington was exploring a region of the valley near where the Battle of Monongahela had taken place. A group of Indians along with an interpreter met the explorers and asked to speak with them. That evening, Washington, his men, and the Indians sat around a fire and the chief told this story.

> I am a chief and ruler over my tribes. My influence extends to the waters of the great lakes, and to the far Blue Mountains. I have traveled a long and weary path, that I might see the young warrior of the great battle. It was on the day, when the white man's blood mixed with the streams of our forest, that I first beheld this chief. I called to my young men and said, 'Mark yon tall and daring warrior? He is not of the red-coat tribe—he hath an Indian's wisdom, and his warriors fight as we do—himself alone is exposed. Quick let your aim be certain, and he dies.' Our rifles were leveled, rifles which, but for him, knew not how to miss. . . . It was all in vain; a power far mightier than we shielded him from harm. He cannot die in battle. I am old, and soon shall be gathered to the great council fire of my fathers in the land of shades, but ere I go, there is something that bids me speak in the voice of prophecy: Listen! The Great Spirit protects that man, and guides his des-

tiny—he will become a chief of nations, and a people yet unborn will hail him as the founder of a mighty empire.[5]

A second account of this conversation notes that the chief himself attempted to kill Washington after pointing him out to his braves. He shot at him not once or twice, but more than fifteen times, and all without effect! With considerable frustration, he finally instructed his braves to stop wasting their ammunition by shooting at him. He finished his discourse with the men around the fire that night by praising Washington and saying, "I am come to pay homage to the man who is the particular favorite of heaven, and who can never die in battle."[4]

Colonel, General , and then President Washington never did die in battle. He passed away quietly at his home at Mt. Vernon in 1799 at the age of sixty-seven. And, as the chief foretold, he had founded a mighty nation.

A Time for
Courage

*Courage is contagious. When a
brave man takes a stand, the
spines of others are often stiffened.*
Billy Graham

*The greatest test of courage is to
bear defeat without
losing heart.*
Robert G. Ingersoll

*The rarest and most admirable
quality of public life, moral
courage.*
Benjamin Disraeli

FLIGHT TO FREEDOM

★

DICK ABEL
BRIG. GEN., USAF (RETIRED)

*It is for freedom that Christ has set us free. Stand firm, then,
and do not let yourselves be burdened again by a yoke of slavery*
(Gal. 5:1 NIV).

*"Therefore if the Son makes you free,
you shall be free indeed"* (John 8:36).

It was a typical, hot sticky day in Vietnam. The humidity always made me feel as though it was about to rain. But as I stood on the tarmac of Gia Lam airport, the heat and humidity barely crossed my mind. My heart sped up in anticipation of meeting men I'd waited and prepared to receive for over three years. But those years at PACOM (Pacific Command) working toward their repatriation were a drop in the bucket compared to years in captivity these men had survived. Two of them had been held for over eight years. It was February 12, 1973, and I'd returned to Vietnam as part of Operation Homecoming to escort our POWs back to freedom.

Negotiations had become serious after the sustained bombing campaign over North Vietnam during Christmas in 1972. For the first time, it appeared the Vietnamese leadership desired to end the war, exchange prisoners, and move forward in the Paris peace negotiations. While there had been so many starts and stops in the process, it felt as though we might actually get there this time.

On that first pickup day, we flew into Hanoi early to prepare to receive American prisoners from the North Vietnamese. In our party were medics, communication experts, mechanics, maintenance personnel, and physicians. We arrived a couple of hours before the scheduled release of the first prisoners and waited in the heat and humidity on the tarmac. Even if the air had not been damp, I'm sure

I would have had sweaty palms.

We received word from our team chief, who had been in negotiations with the North Vietnamese, that the men would be transported to the airport by bus. We called in the first of three C141s that would transport the POWs out of Vietnam. As the 141 taxied into position, an old bus full of anxious Americans pulled up on the tarmac. The negotiating delegations from South Vietnam, France, North Vietnam, and US waited and watched with varied emotions.

I was impressed as the men exited the bus, formed two columns and held their heads high. As I walked the line, I noted quick winks and then a return to solemn faces. One man stepped out of line and held up what appeared to be a handkerchief with Vietnamese writing on it. After a scuffle, he was pushed back into line. My interpreter informed me the offensive words that were written on the handkerchief said, "God bless America."

Then the name of each POW was called. First were eleven of the longest held and then those the North Vietnamese had identified as sick and wounded. As their names were called they came into the changeover area. Each was greeted by the senior air force official, exchanged salutes, and was escorted to the C141.

As they loaded the aircraft, the forty POWs, including three who were in body casts, sat silently on the aircraft. The crew chief and I boarded the aircraft and the ramp was raised. As the last door closed bedlam broke out. Pent-up emotions overflowed as men cried and shared their joy with each other. I will never forget this scene. They hugged each other. They hugged the nurses. After those long years in prison, they hugged everything in sight!

As we flew to Clark Air Base in the Philippines, the senior officer aboard, Captain Jerry Denton, briefed the former prisoners on the events that would soon take place. I sat next to one of the longest held men and asked him how he was captured and how he made it through his captivity. Larry had spent four years in solitary confinement and was tortured extensively. I asked him how he made it through almost eight years of captivity. His answer still burns in my memory; "If it weren't for Jesus Christ, I would have never made it.

When I was walking up and down those muddy hills and they were beating me on my back, I looked up and saw a vision of Jesus. He looked down at me and said, 'Larry, you'll make it. When I climbed the hill, I had a cross on my back.'"

In the next few weeks, I made four more trips to pick up POWs. On my final flight, I escorted prisoners who had been held the shortest time. Their food was better and they had not been tortured. They were able to communicate with each other and had lived in groups. Yet again, as the plane lifted off, the emotions and exuberance were no different than the first flight.

Surprised by their reaction, I sought to discover the reasons behind it. It became clearer when the senior officer shared something that had been written on the wall of the Hanoi Hilton. The words on the wall had no date and no signature. They simply said, "Freedom has a taste to those who fight and almost die that the protected will never know." As I looked around the plane, I realized all these men understood freedom in a way that I might never understand. It's because they had lost their freedom, even just for a few months. Just being in their presence strengthened my own appreciation of my freedoms.

My heart was warmed knowing the Lord allowed me to play a small part in bringing these men to freedom. More than that, I was encouraged to learn that Jesus had been the mainstay for many of them during their hours of darkness.

I returned to my normal duties after I finished escorting the POWs to freedom. Yet, the events of those flights left an indelible imprint on me. When I get discouraged or feel bound up by the challenges and problems of life, I remember how Jesus sustained those who had been imprisoned. I remember the words of Jesus to the captives in chains and I am warmed with encouragement: "You'll make it! When I climbed the hill, I had a cross on my back."

1776 — A Storm, a Wind, and a Fog

★

ABRIDGED FROM *THE LIGHT AND THE GLORY*
BY PETER MARSHALL[5]

USED BY PERMISSION.

Praise the Lord from the earth, You great sea creatures and all ocean depths, Lightning and hail, snow and clouds, stormy winds that do his bidding (Ps. 148:7,8 NIV).

By 1776, the colonists had declared their independence. But that would soon be no more than a useless gesture if the Continental Army couldn't survive. The British had begun to arrive en masse and were attempting to take control of New York to suppress what they considered an uprising. Only one obstacle remained: the American town of Brooklyn New York, at the western end of Long Island.

On the morning of August 22, 15,000 British troops landed on the southeast shore of Brooklyn without opposition. Facing them were barely 8,000 Americans under General George Washington, half of them untrained.

In five days the British had nearly surrounded the Americans just north of the Flatbush region. On August 27 the British gave the order to attack. The Americans' left and center were overwhelmed and fell back to the final defensive perimeter around the northern tip of Brooklyn.

Five times the colonists from Maryland flung themselves at Lord Cornwallis's lines, trying to break through to rescue them. The last time they almost succeeded, but fresh British reinforcements stopped them.

Washington and his generals had observed the entire action through field telescopes. General Washington wrung his hands in anguish and cried out, "Good God, what brave fellows I must this day lose!"

All that afternoon, the Americans held their breath, waiting for the final British assault which would surely finish them. They were outnumbered by more than three to one, low on powder (as always), and would soon have the British fleet in the mouth of the East River at their back.

And so they waited . . . and waited . . . and waited. They never knew that God was with them all the time. For British General Howe, against all military logic, was once again failing to follow up his all-too-obvious advantage. And this was not a dull general! His surrounding maneuver of the night before had been brilliantly conceived and flawlessly executed, taking the Americans entirely by surprise. As afternoon became evening, and the night wore on silently and peacefully, it gradually became apparent that Howe was not going to attack.

The morning of the twenty-eighth dawned overcast and threatening—but quiet; there was still no movement from the British positions. All that day, the Americans continued to wait, tense and exhausted, for the inevitable barrage which would precede the final action. But the British guns remained silent. In the late afternoon, a cold pelting rain began to fall and kept on falling into the night, soaking the tentless, lightly clothed, and hungry Americans. But the rain came on a northeast wind, and that wind prevented Howe's fleet from entering the East River.

And now Washington had a plan. It was a desperate gamble and depended upon so many unlikely intangibles that it hardly deserved to be called a plan. But it was better than a suicidal defense, and surrender was out of the question. If only God's grace continued to favor them . . .

Washington called a council of war and informed his senior officers that he had decided to take the entire army off Brooklyn by small boat. They would rejoin the main body of American forces (some 12,000 additional men) at the foot of Manhattan Island, behind Knox's major batteries. Immediately his generals pointed out that it was a full mile across the East River. All of them knew what the British fleet would do to a flotilla of small boats filled with infantry, the moment they spotted them. Better to die in the trenches—at least there, they could make the British pay dearly.

But Washington had made up his mind. The first thing they needed was boats and men to handle them. By "coincidence," the last reinforcements to have come over from Manhattan were John Glover's company of Marbleheaders. All of these were expert oarsmen, who had practically grown up in small boats on the shores of Massachusetts Bay[1]

All night long these men made the treacherous, two-mile round trip. At first they had to fight the wind and stormy chop. Then, after midnight, the wind died away, so they had to quietly glide through the still waters. Dipping their oars deftly and silently into the water, they pulled them through without a wash and raised them out clean, ready for another stroke.

While the flat calm enabled them to take much heavier loads—so that gunwales were barely above the surface—the danger was much greater now. For there was no storm or rain to cover the accidental noise.

And now came the greatest peril of all: dawn. As the first hints of pink began to illumine the eastern horizon, the embarkation was far from over. At least three more hours would be needed to get the last man across, and the sky above was cloudless. It would be a dazzling, clear day. Now all American eyes were fixed on the eastern sky as it began to redden and the darkness shrank westward. Though the men remained silent, one could sense their anxiety mounting as the covering of night began to recede and leave them naked.

What happened next should be told by one who saw it: "As the dawn of the next day approached," Major Ben Tallmadge would write, "those of us who remained in the trenches became very anxious for our own safety, and when the dawn appeared there were several regiments still on duty. At this time, a very dense fog began to rise (out of the ground and off the river), and it seemed to settle in a peculiar manner over both encampments. I recollect this peculiar providential occurrence perfectly well, and so very dense was the atmosphere that I could scarcely discern a man at six yards distance . . . we tarried until the sun had risen, but the fog remained as dense as ever."

Virtually every man who kept a diary that day recorded that fog, and most of them made a point of giving the credit where it was due. The fog remained intact until the last boat, with Washington in it, had departed. Then it lifted, and the shocked British ran to the shore and started firing after them, but they were out of range. Nearly 8,000 men had been extricated from certain death or imprisonment without the loss of a single life!

The Continental Army had suffered a severe defeat, with some 1,500 casualties. Yet, thanks to a storm, a wind, and a fog, and too many human "coincidences" to number, there still was a Continental Army!

MIGHTIER THAN THE HURRICANE

★

LT. CHRISTOPHER L. PESILE
USN

Your throne, O Lord, has been established from time immemorial. You yourself are from the everlasting past. The mighty oceans have roared, O Lord. The mighty oceans roar like thunder; the mighty oceans roar as they pound the shore. But mightier than the violent raging of the seas, mightier than the breakers on the shore — the Lord above is mightier than these! (Ps. 93: 2-4 NLT).

"Now set Helo Flight Quarters," came the announcement. "No way, not in this sea state," I said to the other two pilots I was with on the USS *John F. Kennedy*. We had gone up there to look out at the angry seas churned up by Hurricane Floyd. My helicopter squadron had seven helicopters aboard for Hurricane Evacuation. We had been underway several days to escape the coming storm.

We hadn't flown since departing; however, on an early September morning, we received an urgent request for help from Coast Guard Station Miami. They had picked up a distress call around 7:30 A.M. from the oceangoing tugboat *Gulf Majesty*. The tugboat was foundering in heavy seas approximately three hundred miles off the coast of Jacksonville, Florida. The caller reported eight people were abandoning ship into a fifteen-man life raft.

During the flight brief, I remember praying and asking God to protect those men in the raft long enough for us to get there. The deteriorating weather conditions caused me to pray for our protection as well. The heavy seas broke over the sixty-foot bow of our ship and swept eight of our own life rafts out to sea.

Later that morning, after the carrier had closed to within 130 miles of the last known position, we took off. Our rescue team consisted of two helicopters with crews of two pilots, a hoist operator, and a rescue swimmer.

Seventy miles from the ship, we lost radio contact. But as we closed on the rescue position we spotted some debris in the water. The winds were greater than fifty knots pushing up twenty to twenty-five foot seas, about the height of a two-story building.

One of my crewmen spotted three survivors in the water who had just popped orange smoke. We marked their position with marine smoke and got out of the way as the lead aircraft, *Dash One*, came in to do the pickup. After picking up these three survivors, lead informed us there were still five more survivors out there somewhere. We executed a search of the immediate area, but after thirty minutes we were forced to return to the carrier to refuel.

We took off again in the early afternoon flying to where we thought the remaining survivors might be, based on the prevailing winds and previous location of survivors. As we approached the position the weather began to deteriorate as I descended from 1,000 feet to 500 feet and then to 300 feet. The winds were now at fifty-five knots (sixty mph) and the seas a nightmarish thirty feet.

During this second rescue, I felt the Lord's guiding hand upon me. As I approached a thunder cell, I circled around it, cleared the weather, and spotted the 750-foot barge the tugboat had been pulling before it sank. Had I flown the other way around the thunderstorm, we never would have spotted that barge. We circled it several times and determined it was abandoned.

We searched carefully because a little life raft wouldn't last long in thirty-foot seas and fifty-five-knot winds. It had been a long day already and it would be dark soon. Both rescue crews were reaching their limits. This would be the last rescue attempt of the day.

After asking the Lord for guidance, I made the decision to search for the raft back upwind toward that morning's survivor pickup point. I figured a barge broadside to the wind would blow farther than a small raft with a sea anchor.

We were in and out of the driving rainstorm as we searched. Visibility varied from three miles to less than one-eighth of a mile at times. After forty-five minutes of exhausting flying and desperate searching, I'd reached the limits of my skill and training to find the survivors. I prayed again for God's help. I realized nothing short of divine intervention would be required to find them in this weather. The visibility had deteriorated to the equivalent of looking through your windshield during a car wash. Ten minutes later we received our miracle. I flew over the raft and my co-pilot yelled, "On top! On top!" We dropped a smoke marker, turned around, and began to hover.

I thought flying the search pattern was difficult, but it paled in comparison to hovering a helicopter in these conditions. My copilot had to back me up on instruments since I couldn't see the horizon and my automatic flight control system, which helps stabilize the helicopter, kept kicking off. The radar altimeter kept shifting thirty feet as huge waves came under the aircraft. There were a few calls from my copilot and the hoist operator telling me to watch my altitude as we flew dangerously close to the water.

For a few minutes I didn't think it would be possible to stay in the hover. I desperately prayed for help as my heart pounded and sweat poured down my face. I remember watching in awe from sixty feet up as the rescue swimmer repeatedly battled his way through those huge waves to the raft to rescue the survivors. I asked the Lord to watch over them and give them strength. I prayed for the safety of our aircraft. One by one we lifted the survivors from the deadly sea. After thirty-five minutes, and what seemed like an eternity at the time, the crew chief informed me all five were aboard. None seriously injured.

In interviews with the three survivors from the first rescue, we found out they had been in the water for over four hours being pummeled by those twenty-five foot seas. They prayed to the Lord to help them stay together and almost immediately after that prayer, one of them felt a tap on the shoulder. He looked and found a broomstick from the wreckage. That was the only thing that had kept them together through their ordeal. Toward the end of the four hours, they once again prayed for a miracle as they neared the end of their strength and hypothermia began to set in. One of the survivors said, "I never saw helicopters coming to get us, I only saw two angels from heaven sent to deliver us."

A Time
to Trust

Put your trust in God, my boys,
but mind to keep your powder dry.
Oliver Cromwell

And this be our motto,
"In God is our trust."
Francis Scott Key

Trust ivrybody—but cut th' ca-ards.
Finley Peter Dunne

Trusting in Him who can go with me,
and remain with you,
and be everywhere for good,
let us confidently hope
that all will yet be well.
Abraham Lincoln

CARRIER LANDING GONE BAD

★

MIKE NEWMAN
COMMANDER USN (RETIRED)

Those who go down to the sea in ships,
Who do business on great waters;
They have seen the works of the Lord,
And His wonders in the deep. . . .
Their soul melted away in their misery. . . .
Then they cried to the Lord in their trouble,
And He brought them out of their distresses.
(Ps. 107: 23, 24, 26b, 28 NASB)

Ever heard the term "party animal"? I was the poster child in the early 1970s. When I came back from Vietnam in 1971, I felt I had earned every minute of pleasure and relaxation I could give myself. I had served on the USS *Iwo Jima* in the waters off Vietnam and was glad to be in friendly waters again. I just didn't know I was about to get more friendly with water than I ever could have wished for.

Though I didn't know Him, God was about to get my attention. I was flying my final trap in a TA-4 *Skyhawk* to the aircraft carrier USS *Lexington*. A trap is an arrested landing where the aircraft's tail hook catches one of four wires stretched across the landing area of the carrier. I had completed my final trap landing safely and heard the great words, "That's your final trap, you're qualified."

At that point, I was directed over toward the catapult. All that remained was one more take-off and an easy landing ashore. I was looking forward to a night of celebration and partying to rival any previous nights. I had earned it! The deck crew member gave me a signal to turn and nothing happened. I pressed the nose wheel steering button again without result.

Either the nose wheel steering had stopped working or the nose wheel was cocked out of limits. I stepped on my brakes and I heard them clank uselessly on the floor.

I pumped them and got a little brake pressure, but it wasn't going to be enough.

I was headed over to the edge of the carrier deck.

At this point I had two choices and only five seconds to decide what to do. I could eject from the cockpit or ride it over the side. The deck was sixty feet above the water with some netting on a cat-walk along the edge.

At that time we had the old Martin-Baker seats that ejected you with an artillery shell. Human cannon ball stuff. I'd seen a lot of people hurt ejecting in situations like this and thought I'd take my chances going over the side. My guess was I'd get tangled up in the catwalk and netting along the edge of the carrier. That way I could be rescued without risking the ejection seat or the water. Fat chance!

The *Lexington* weighed about 60,000 tons, all of it steel, and it was going about twenty-five knots (thirty mph). I had one last look at blue sky and then the plane nosed over the side. My hope of catching the netting vanished as the plane did a perfect ten into the green water. Falling sixty feet took only a couple of seconds and the plane went in like a knife. If it had belly-flopped, the impact would have killed me.

My mind raced as I sank into the water. Then suddenly, miraculously, this 25,000 pound jet began to rise from the depths like a kid's toy in a bathtub. Moments later I was astonished to see daylight streaming through the canopy (My plane was low on fuel by the time I did my fifth trap, so there was a lot of air in the fuel tanks).

I pulled one lever and my canopy exploded off the fuselage and another lever cut the straps that held me in my seat. I stood up to freedom before realizing I was snagged on a line that should have been cut. Water rushed into the canopy and the plane began to sink.

I jerked the straps once more—free! Almost.

I swam away from the carrier as best I could but the sinking plane managed to hit me in the back of the helmet. Dazed, I pushed away from the tail to keep from being entangled and began swimming harder to escape the undertow of the carrier's wake. If I weren't quick enough or far enough away I'd be pulled under.

The next sound I heard was the beating of helicopter blades as the rescue aircraft hovered over me.

I came away from my ordeal without injury, but a spiritual journey had just begun.

My brush with death put me on a path of discovery to find the meaning of my life. Almost dying three times in a matter of minutes has a way of doing that.

I began asking everyone I knew whether they believed in God, heaven, or hell—my friends thought I'd gone crazy.

But I didn't care. I was seeking something that could satisfy the inner questions awakened in me, and I wasn't going to stop until I found it.

It was two years later that I came to the end of my search in the person of Jesus Christ, and I have never been the same since.

Today, I help others on that journey as well.

Whether I'm working with young men and women through Officer's Christian Fellowship or at the local prison ministering to convicts, I rejoice in the work He's done in my life since that day I went into the water.

I'm retired from the Navy now and my days of making white-knuckle carrier landings are behind me.

In Christ, however, I believe the excitement has just begun.

FAITH IN FLIGHT

★

MAJOR KEVIN DAILEY
USAF

So do not fear, for I am with you; do not be dismayed,
for I am your God. I will strengthen you and help you;
I will uphold you with my righteous right hand. (Is. 41: 10, NIV).

It was on a late winter flight in 1993 that I came to a deeper under-standing of God's grace. I was the navigator on an RC-135 (recon-naissance aircraft) mission out of the Kingdom of Saudi Arabia and faced a standard redeployment back home: two air refuelings, mul-tiple navigation legs, and a lengthy trip across the pond to our home base in Nebraska. This flight started out uneventfully enough and after completing our second air refueling, we coasted out of the United Kingdom and into the Atlantic.

So do not fear

We had been flying for several hours and were about halfway across the Atlantic Ocean. Looking down at the #1 generator gauge, I began to notice it fluctuating—first mildly and then wildly. Within seconds, the generator disintegrated. While this wasn't good, it was-n't serious enough to get overly worried. But within a very short time, our two remaining generators went off-line and then failed. We had no generator power. This definitely wasn't good.

Things began to go from bad to worse. As we sat in the dark, we realized the #1 constant speed drive overheat light had just come on as well. To keep an engine fire from developing, we shut down the #1 engine.

I am with you

We were three hours from landfall and all of our awesome elec-trical systems were reduced to one aircraft battery the size of a shoebox! Power available now was barely sufficient to sustain us. As I looked at our navigation system to determine our position, the entire system went off-line—the victim of inadequate power.

Without highly accurate computers, I turned back to the training I'd received long ago using the old compass and sextant. Much like Magellan centuries before, I tracked our position across the sky using the stars. The only difference was that at 35,000 feet we were traveling twenty-five times faster than he did. Our crew of thirty-five turned to their duties. Many of us also turned to the Lord as we thought about the very real possibility of a winter ditching in the freezing North Atlantic waters. That scenario, if we survived the impact, meant about twenty minutes of life before freezing. I just knew God hadn't forgotten us. "God won't leave us now," I whispered. It was my prayer of faith.

I will strengthen you and help you

All of us onboard were professionals and approached our problems calmly in spite of ever diminishing alternatives. We wanted to maximize our survival in the event we ditched. Meanwhile we pointed the aircraft to the nearest safe landing field. While Newfoundland was closer, it had whiteout conditions from a snowstorm. Our next alternative was Goose Bay, Labrador, in northeast Canada. As we got closer to Canadian landfall, we had to descend to stay both visual and out of icing conditions. Without electrical power, we didn't have the ability to use our anti-ice systems which put us in a very dangerous flying condition.

I will uphold you

I sat in the jump seat doing visual navigation as we approached land. Through the intermittent clouds, I saw the Goose Bay inlet. Closer and closer we came. Finally, we crossed over land and our hearts jumped for joy. Our emergency radio did not work initially— "Mayday, Mayday, Mayday—this is *Snoop 46* on guard," I called. Switching the aircraft battery on for a brief moment, the copilot called on guard and picked up a Canadian C-130. "Thank you God," we all whispered. He passed us to a Canadian approach controller. He immediately climbed us 3,000 feet as we were below the minimum safe altitude for the sector. God had been with us again.

With my righteous right hand

As we dumped extra gas in preparation to land, it was still a bit unnerving as there was no way to read our electrically driven fuel panel. How much fuel did we have? What was our burn rate? Were our tanks balanced or was our aircraft in danger of landing out of balance and out of control? There was no way to know other than by roughly estimating our burn rates.

Our major concern was if we landed too heavy, we might not be able to stop before running off the runway. We could have survived all that happened to still not survive the landing. It was a sobering thought as the pilot dropped the landing gear, and I confirmed it was down and locked. I counted the gear and confirmed my finding. "That's three down and locked," and the pilot nodded.

The approach controller gave us perfect vectors as we came down final. The pilot flared and the heavy jet touched down on the wet runway. We screamed down the runway as the pilot fought to keep the nosewheel on centerline. The "runway remaining" markers flew by us—8,000 feet remaining, 7,000, 6,000. The two pilots using all their leg strength, pressed their combined weights against the metal brake pedals trying to bring the jet to a stop. 5,000, 4,000, 3,000 remaining. Were we too heavy? The pilot's jaw clenched as the 2,000 foot marker passed and the runway overrun came into view. 1,000 feet and the brakes were finally having their full effect. Less than one thousand feet before the overrun, the jet lurched and finally settled on the runway—dead stopped with a razor's edge of runway to spare. We had made it!

As we taxied to park, the entire field was hit with a massive blowing snow creating complete whiteout conditions. It was at that point when the entire situation hit me. One half hour later and we couldn't have landed at the last airfield we had fuel to reach. The cold Atlantic would have been our only choice that winter's eve. I bowed my head and heart to the unseen hand that saved us that night.

MILITARY LIFE — THROUGH A CHILD'S EYES

★

KJERSTIN S. O'LEARY
USAF MILITARY DEPENDENT

When I was a child, I spoke as a child, I understood as a child, I thought as a child; but when I became a man, I put away childish things. For now we see in a mirror, dimly, but then face to face. Now I know in part, but then I shall know just as I also am known (1 Cor. 13:11,12).

I never understood the point of hopscotch. *Toss. Jump. One foot. Two feet. Turn. Pick up the rock. Don't fall! Repeat.* No great thrill. Maybe I never liked the game because it seemed too much like my childhood.

Being a military kid, or a "brat" as we're sometimes called, gave me the opportunity to have a lot of mixed blessings and experiences. The appearance of the moving van seemed like the half-empty glass—left behind dreams, friendships and roots. I didn't see the opportunities that awaited me through the windshield of our car as we left our neighborhood for the last time. Rather, I saw the missed possibilities disappearing through the rear view mirror.

Arriving in the new neighborhood I felt very much alone. I walked to school to the sounds of my own feet, kicking stray rocks on the sidewalk. Two of my soon-to-be classmates walked along, hand in hand on the other side of the street. With their perky ponytails swishing back and forth, they chatted and laughed in the morning sun, walking to the same school their mothers attended before them. Their life was so simple: planned, perfect. They were blessed to grow up in one place with people who would know them from cradle to grave. My vision blurred once again and I cried out to my one friend. "Jesus, when I grow up, I want to live in the same place with the same people my entire life. I want to be happy." I prayed this prayer every day that year. It was everything I thought I would ever want.

Third grade was the worst. Standing at the head of the class was that stern, yet soft, teacher we always talked about. Do you remember me? Where am I? Look in the corner... there, in the back. The little girl biting her lower lip and wiping her clammy hands on her corduroy pants. I'm the new kid in school. I'm always the new kid. Don't bother getting to know me, I'll soon be gone again. Gone and forgotten.

I got used to it over time, but elementary school was particularly lonely. What I remember most was walking to and from school — alone. Time and again, I tried to break into the cliques and "friends-for-life" circles. My classmates felt sorry for me. They pitied me, and I pitied myself.

In the years that followed, my prayer went unanswered and seemingly unheard. My father's career whisked me into the heart of the Middle East where I finished sixth grade. I began junior high under the shadow of Pike's Peak in Colorado and finished on a small colonial island in New England. I began and finished high school in a series of southern and midwestern cities. Between moving trucks and oceans of brown packing paper, there was California, Alaska, Nebraska, Egypt, Israel, Colorado, Alabama, Nebraska (again), and Rhode Island. All in all, during my youth I lived in fourteen different cities and attended eleven different schools.

I used to wonder, "How can God say He loves His children when He doesn't answer their prayers?" And I grew angry because I couldn't control the game. I moved whenever the air force moved my Dad. It seemed so unfair.

Years later, I returned to one of our many homes. Now a grown woman, I bumped into someone who still remembered me from that lonely third grade year. It was the same pony-tailed girl I once watched and envied on the way to school. She still lived in the same neighborhood, had the same friends, and knew practically everything about everybody who lived there. As I listened to her, I realized that her world was far different and seemed smaller than mine. We chatted for a little while and then said our good-byes. I got into my car, closed the door, and rested my head on the steering wheel. *Is that what I was wishing for all those years?*

I drove away thinking, hard. We were a family who had marched to the military's tune—*jump, jump, turn . . . repeat*. But until now, I never realized I actually enjoyed the "leaping" part of life. I held warm memories of the games we played in the back of the minivan as we ventured from one coast to the other. For so long I had thought I was being cheated out of the good things in life. I had blamed God for not giving me what I wanted, when He lovingly gave me what I needed. Certainly, there were a lot of difficulties growing up in a family that moved every twenty-four months for twenty years. Yet, for the first time, I felt blessed to have experienced so many cultures and countries in my short life. The days of shopping in London, eating hummus in Syria, riding camels in Cairo, and climbing the pyramids of Giza all came rushing back.

It was time to go. I boarded another plane to begin yet another adventure. But this one was different. This one was of my own choosing. A summer in Paris was before me and I thought how much I loved my life. My little girl wishes and prayers had long since vanished like the morning mist.

Looking back, I know God really did hear my prayers. But instead of listening to my words, He listened to my heart. No, I won't live around friends who remember me when I was seven, or play in a treehouse my grandfather built. But I no longer pity myself. The world became my house and heaven my final destination. And, wherever I find myself, I know I can always find a road that will lead me home.

EGYPT!...INSTEAD OF HAWAII?

★

RENEE REILLY
US ARMY WIFE

Then Job answered, "Even today my complaint is bitter. . .But He knows the way that I take; When he has tested me, I shall come forth as gold" Job 23: 2,10 (NKJV).

Last spring I was very angry with God. My husband, Dan, knew he would be going overseas, and he had lined up a job in Hawaii. We were excited at the thought of an island tour. Our excitement quickly disappeared after he spoke with the assignment officer. He was informed he was not going to Hawaii with his family, but to Egypt alone! To add further insult, his unaccompanied remote tour would begin within 60 days.

All year I had prayed for a miracle to keep our family together, not caring where we went as long as we were together. Dan and I had never fared very well apart, and I was fearful of what a year of separation would do to us. When I realized there would be no miracle to keep us together, I wondered why God hadn't listened and acted. Wasn't I worthy? Wasn't my family important? I was really angry and didn't really want to know a God who I thought had turned His back on my family.

My heart just wasn't into hearing Him or being excited for others' blessings. I turned to Him once more and told Him I didn't think I could do this. I didn't want to do this. But if I must, please don't let me do it alone. Please, I prayed, send me a companion or a neighbor. I needed someone I could talk to, lean on, laugh with and cry with.

I watched my dear husband and my dear friends pack up and leave from Command and General Staff College (CGSC). I was left behind. Why? The Word seemed to tell me, "If we are faithless, He will remain faithful, for He cannot disown Himself." (2 Tim 2:13)

I went home for a month over the summer. My sister-in-law gave me a series of books by Tim LaHaye and Jerry Jenkins. They really spoke to my heart. As I read, I began to question my faith and my knowledge of who God truly is. I realized I knew very little and I wanted to know more.

When I returned home, the neighborhood had filled up with the next class of CGSC students and their families. Forty couples and 113 children surrounded me, yet I still felt alone. I was seeking in others what I should have been seeking in God—companionship. I had been waiting for God to single me out, to "come near to me," in spite of the fact that I was not willing to "draw near to Him" with a true heart (James 4:8).

I began attending our neighborhood Bible study, even though it was motivated by my sense of correct "protocol." I thought I should do this if I wanted to know God. Never in my wildest dreams did I expect to be so richly blessed! That summer I finally cried out to God and laid my anger on His shoulders. I surrendered myself, my control over my life, and my ideas of "protocol." I simply focused on Him.

I believe that one of the reasons Dan and I have been separated this year is so I would turn to God. He wanted to become my companion—the companion I had longed for—so that I could survive my year of marital separation. He showed me I didn't have to face a year alone.

God blessed me with the comfort of the Holy Spirit and, through my neighborhood Bible study, a support group of true friends. He blessed my children with good friends from the children of my Bible study group. He gave Dan a Christian roommate and co-worker who became his accountability partner. Despite the miles of separation, our relationship flourished.

Each of us grew both spiritually and emotionally. I'm certain that this would not have occurred if we had been together that year. I remember studying a Scripture passage I had read many times before. The difference when I read it this time was that the Holy Spirit showed me how to apply it to my life. The difference was, I listened.

"'For I know the plans that I have for you,' declares the Lord, 'plans for welfare and not for calamity to give you a future and a hope.' Then you will call upon Me and come and pray to Me, and I will listen to you. And you will seek Me and find Me, when you search for Me with all your heart" (Jeremiah 29:11-13, NASB).

The passage has new meaning to me now. It gave me strength and great hope as I discovered that God was faithful. I learned I could trust Him even when I wanted Hawaii and He said, "Egypt." Yes, I learned to trust Him even when I couldn't understand Him.

(Editors note: Dan and Renee Reilly were assigned to Hawaii following Dan's remote tour to Egypt.)

(Used by permission of Command magazine, published by Officers' Christian Fellowship, Englewood, Colorado.)

A TIME
TO WEEP

I did not weep;
I had turned to stone inside
Dante

Jesus wept
John 11:35

Why can I not weep?
Napoleon

PASSOVER AND PROMOTION

★

MAJOR CONNER BROWN
US ARMY

For not from the east, nor from the west,
Nor from the desert comes exaltation, But God is the Judge;
He puts down one, and exalts another (Ps. 75:6-7 NASB).

The military has a system of promotion that we call "up or out." For officers, this up-or-out decision point comes after about eleven years of service. At that point, officers are evaluated for promotion to major. If you're promoted, you move on. If not, you're given one additional chance and then you're involuntarily separated from the service. There is no such thing as a vested retirement system—no 401k, just a severance check as you go out the door. If you don't make it to twenty years, you're out of luck.

I was about to meet this significant promotion point and visited my branch in Washington DC to learn where I stood. My branch manager had this stark assessment, "I recommend you take the money and run. I don't believe you'll make major." My heart sank, even though I had to admit my record was weak.

Due to downsizing, the army was offering officers a special severance payment of $200,000 to encourage us to leave the service. However, if I remained and failed to be promoted twice I'd be separated and given only $44,000. It was a difference of more than $150,000. Because I was the only officer in my branch-year group who had not commanded a company, my chances for promotion were slim.

I asked a good Christian friend, Jay George, who was also a branch manager, to look over my record and give me a second opinion. Jay told me the same thing. I asked, "What should I do?"

He said, "Pray for promotion if that's what you want, but I'd also pray not to become bitter if passed over."

I was devastated. I had dedicated my life to serving my country.

I'd spent a great deal of my life away from my family in difficult and dangerous circumstances. *After ten years, is it over?* I began praying immediately. The first words out of my mouth were, "Why, Lord?" The subway trip back to my motel room was the longest ride I ever took. It was one of the lowest points of my army career and Christian life.

That night I began earnestly praying and seeking God's guidance as I read through Psalms and Proverbs. I came upon Proverbs 28:1, which I would hold onto by my fingernails for the next twenty-seven months. "The wicked flee when no one is pursuing, But the righteous are as bold as the lion." (NASB) It would be the verse that would keep me in the army. I sensed God telling me, "Conner Brown, I have you right where I want you. Stay where you are."

As summer rolled into fall, twenty-five of sixty-five officers in my branch year group left the army. I thought perhaps I would be promoted by default, but God had bigger things in store. He was preparing my heart to receive a miracle, if I was willing to go the distance. Many officers resigned from fear of pass-over or for the $200,000 separation bonus. Instead, I stood by Proverbs 28:1. I had not come into the Army for money, nor would I be enticed to leave for money. I would stay.

In the midst of waiting, I deployed to Bosnia for Operation Joint Endeavor and endured a seven-month separation from my wife. Lin was pregnant with our first child, so it was a difficult time for us. Three days after I returned from Bosnia, the army released the results of the majors' board. I had been passed over. I felt humiliated, as if ten years of my life had been wasted and thrown away. My acting battalion commander called me in to break the news.

She asked, "What are you going to do?" When I didn't respond, she continued, "You know your promotion chances for next year are zero percent. You might as well get out."

Lin, now seven months pregnant, was waiting for me in the car. She could hardly believe the news. She had been praying and was sure I would be promoted. We took a walk that evening around the battalion area and it meant so much to me when she said, "I still love you anyway."

Thinking I would soon get out of the army, my unit decided not to deploy me again. This "blessing" allowed me to see my son Conner born. I received a lot of guidance I didn't ask for: *"You need to get out and get a job." "You should just rack this up as a failure and get on with your life." "Don't you realize how you're stressing out your family?"* Instead of quitting, I decided I would stay for another look. Anywhere from zero to nine percent would be promoted "above the zone."

The day before the decision deadline my branch manager called and frantically asked why I had not sent in my resignation paperwork. He said, "Why are you doing this? You're just wasting your time."

Since most of my battalion was in Bosnia, I was the acting battalion S-3. My self-esteem was at an all-time low. I had difficulty working through self-pity and depression. In addition, past mistakes I made kept popping into my mind. I also had to deal with anger over treatment from former bosses. Just going to work was hard, especially watching captains in my unit being frocked to major.

I met weekly with Dave Coffield, an area minister. I told Dave how God had spoken to me and asked, "Dave, I feel like such a fool. Did I really hear God? I was so certain."

Dave was one of the few people who encouraged me. He said, "I think you'll be a major. Somehow, some way, God will keep you in the army."

"How, Dave? It will have to be a miracle. I only have about four or five good efficiency reports in my whole record; the average captain has ten or twelve."

Dave replied, "You could have none. If God wants to keep you in the army, and I believe He does, He doesn't need good reports. That way He gets all the glory."

I went to see a former rater to ask his help in having a report removed from my file. He refused, and my record went before the board with the same black mark. I think it was God's way of showing me that the battle belonged to Him. As with Gideon, God increased the odds so much, that only He could receive the glory if promotion occurred.

A few months before the release of the board results, I was unexpectedly deployed to Europe. It was a stressful time to be overseas. I felt all along that God had brought me into the Army, so I decided only God could remove me. However, it was not until He sent me to Germany in those last months of waiting that I came to peace with God about my future. If He wanted me to be a civilian, I was willing to go where He would take me.

I returned from Germany four days before the majors' list was released. Late on an August afternoon, my boss came into my office. He asked one of my NCOs to leave. My heart was in my throat. He closed the door and said, "I just want to let you know, you made it." I immediately started crying.

He said, "Hey man, what's wrong? You made it."

I said, "You don't understand, sir. God just performed a miracle."

I immediately called my wife. I said, "Honey, I'll be a little late coming home from work. I have to stop at clothing sales and buy some oak leaves (major's rank)." She paused for a moment, then started weeping and shouting, "Praise the Lord!" I was the only "above-the-zone" officer in my branch selected and one of eleven in the entire army.

I deployed to Sarajevo that October and was promoted to major there at the end of January. God had placed me exactly where He wanted me and by His grace I was promoted. My contemporaries may trust in their records and accomplishments, but I have learned to trust in my Lord Jesus Christ. Promotions, I have learned, come not from men, but from His almighty hand. *"Some boast in chariots, and some in horses; But we will boast in the name of the Lord our God"* (Ps. 20:7 NASB).

(Used by permission of Command magazine, published by Officers' Christian Fellowship, Englewood, Colorado.)

A Prison Called Leavenworth

★

Rejoice with those who rejoice, and weep with those who weep (Rom. 12:15).

I was sick and you visited Me;
I was in prison and you came to Me (Matt. 25:36).

I've held three commands in my career, and each one was completely different. There were a lot of high points along the way, and there were at least as many low points. After three commands, I knew I'd had enough. It was time to do something else and there wasn't much point in looking back. One of the low points of my final command was having to escort a fellow officer, under guard, to Ft. Leavenworth Military Prison.

I was commanding a flying squadron and was at my desk late in the afternoon when the phone rang. A voice said firmly, "This is Agent Baylor from the Office of Special Investigations (OSI). I'd like to meet you tomorrow at the Wing Commander's office. Can you be there?" I nodded my head and then realized I was on the phone. I managed a barely audible, "Yes, I'll be there."

I hung up the phone and tried to figure out what this was all about. Even as a squadron commander, I'd only been to the Wing Commander's office once, and very briefly. Finally, I got a little mad and called the agent back, "Is this about me or one of the people who works for me?" He was embarrassed and said, "Oh no, sir, it's about one of your people, but I can't talk about it until tomorrow." Somewhat relieved, somewhat troubled, I hung up the phone.

The next morning as I neared the door of the Wing Commander's office, two men in suits stepped out. One introduced himself without extending his hand, "Hi, I'm Agent Willis. I'm with the FBI." Right then and there I think I started going into shock. I sat in a chair in front of the Wing Commander with my boss, an FBI agent, and an OSI agent. The agent started by swearing us to secrecy, declaring a lapse in confidentiality was a felony and punishable by— well, you get the picture.

The FBI agent pulled out a stack of photographs indicating an officer of mine, Joe Canby*⁶ had been caught in the commission of serious felonies. When they passed the photos to me, I looked swiftly at only the first photo and my stomach churned. I passed them to my boss sitting beside me.

I tried to assess the impact of this situation and could only conclude it was going to be bad. Joe was popular among his peers and had served many years in the service. I knew the FBI would arrest him soon, his life would be ruined, and the morale of the squadron would plummet. The man's wife and children would suffer as well.

A week later the FBI had gathered all the evidence they believed they needed and knocked on his door. The news spread like wildfire when the newspapers reported the arrest. The phone began to ring off the hook with questions. However, as a commander I had to respect the privacy of the individual. I called my squadron together and told them the news of Joe's arrest and the publicly releasable facts. Unfortunately, the facts didn't fill in the gaps, and speculation ruled the day. A number of people surmised I had a vendetta against him or had set him up. I couldn't answer those charges because to do so would have violated his legal privacy rights.

The process of criminal justice has been described as a grinding wheel that moves slowly and surely. Along the way there is a lot of pain. It took nearly a year before Joe came to trial. During that time, the squadron suffered through the under-the-surface tension I expected. Nevertheless, we had an important mission to accomplish and we did it. When the trial ended, he was found guilty and sentenced to serve time at Ft. Leavenworth Military Prison in Kansas. Over the months between arrest and trial, I had spent a lot of time with him and managed to guide him into counseling with various sources. The day after he was sentenced, I was asked to provide an escort to take him to prison. It had to be someone of equal or higher rank. I could have sent someone else, but I didn't. I felt it was a responsibility I had to bear.

The trip started out in a somewhat lighthearted way. Joe, now a former officer, was a convict. Yet he told jokes and made funny remarks throughout the first half of the trip. I couldn't figure out how he could be lighthearted when his wife and children were home crying, and his career had ended in disgrace. I had to give this former comrade in arms credit for trying to keep up a brave front. But as we drew closer to Kansas, and then to the small town of Ft. Leavenworth, the conversation came to a halt altogether.

As we approached the prison, its massive structure was visible even from a distance. I was overcome by the historic nature of the brick and stone fortress. The building was nearly two hundred years old and even the prison cells were opened with skeleton keys, artifacts of another era. The main prison fortress was about eight stories in all, three stories of which were below ground. It was octagonal in shape, made of brick and was both dark and formidable.

We pulled into the parking lot. We walked into the reception area and reported to the guard at the entrance with the prisoner, who was in handcuffs. He ushered Joe into an alcove where he ordered him to strip. After the first of what would be three strip searches was completed, we walked with the prison guard and the prisoner into the inner prison. Joe was taken to the deepest bowels of the prison where he was in-processed. Though it got hotter and hotter as we descended, no cool breeze or air conditioning made the journey more comfortable. In the 1800s there was no air conditioning, and things hadn't improved much since then.

Finally, we reached the area of his cellblock, and my responsibility ended. I signed over the prisoner to the guard and said good-bye. I promised to return to visit when the first visiting day came and later kept my promise. The trip home was long and silent.

It's so easy and enjoyable to rejoice with those who rejoice. As a commander, I enjoyed the promotion parties and visiting new parents and their babies in the hospital. Yet, sometimes we are asked to suffer with those who suffer and weep with those who weep. Too often Christians have a tendency to abandon the wounded rather than minister to them. I think we grow in ways not easily seen when we touch the face of pain and don't draw back.

When I think of Joe, I can't bring myself to feel better or more righteous than he. I wouldn't try to excuse what he did, but I also know I've made my share of mistakes. While I *am* convinced he was treated justly, I am also convinced that except for God's grace, I would be no better off. Maybe that's why I walk a little more carefully during each new day God gives me. The morning sky and evening sunset are as precious to me as the grace He poured out freely at Calvary.

A FRIEND CLOSER
THAN A BROTHER

★

LT. COL. JAMES V. "CUFF" KELSO
USAF

A friend loves at all times,
and a brother is born for adversity (Prov.17:17, NIV).

I first met Ted when we were both cadets at the Air Force Academy. He was truly a late 60s "free spirit." We had a lot of fun together and had some wild adventures skiing in the Rockies and shooting the rapids on the Arkansas River a week before we graduated. Our aim at this point was like the gum commercial: "double your pleasure, double your fun." Whatever else we did, we didn't want to be bored.

Following our graduation in the summer of 1968, we headed off to pilot training at Laredo, Texas. Along with another friend, we traveled south "flying" our cars in tight formation down the highways of Colorado, New Mexico, and Texas. We envisioned ourselves as we'd soon be, in high-speed jet fighters. Four-lane roads were best because then we could spread out into a diamond formation, just like the Thunderbirds.

Ted and I were roommates in the Bachelor Officers Quarters (BOQ) and led the life of young, single bachelors. We bought a boat, dated a lot, traveled when we could, camped on the beach, and lived a fairly carefree life. Yet, in the back of our minds was achieving that ultimate goal—becoming military pilots. That dream was realized a year later in August 1969 when we both walked across the stage to receive our pilot wings.

Our military experience was colored by the green tapestry of Vietnam. Both of us flew over the jungles, not in jets, as we had both envisioned, but in old, leaky, propeller-driven aircraft. Ted was assigned as a forward air controller (FAC) flying the O-2, while I flew a C-7A Caribou, supporting special forces camps via dirt runways.

Despite our disappointment we both had an exciting, exhausting year. While we were separated by aircraft type and base, we managed to hook up one day while airborne. I'd been monitoring the tactical frequency when I heard his distinctive voice coming across the radio over Pleiku in the Central Highlands.

For me, Vietnam was a series of highs and lows. Both Ted and I lost friends we'd known since our Academy days. Additionally, we seemed to sustain a series of losses from each of our units to enemy fire.

During this same period, a friend in my squadron persistently witnessed to me about Jesus Christ. God finally got through to me and I became a believer.

I managed to survive my tour and returned to the states. God provided a marvelous surprise gift for me as I prepared to board my Freedom Bird to McChord AFB. There boarding the plane with me was my best friend, Ted. Together we'd come and together we left.

From the time we lifted off the runway at Cam Ranh Bay until we touched down on American soil, we never stopped talking. I was being assigned to the Air Force Academy as a T-41 flight instructor while Ted felt the call for more adventure. He volunteered for a second tour in Vietnam in a classified FAC program. We talked about our futures, then bid each other farewell.

My bachelor days came to an abrupt end while I was at the Academy, and I wished Ted could have been present for that special day. I wanted him to meet the woman who became my wonderful wife. Two years after we parted company, I was flying T-38s and Ted was still in combat. He'd taken on the assignment of hunting down North Vietnamese troops moving south through Laos and Cambodia.

It was a phone call to our tiny base housing duplex in Georgia that brought news that stunned me. Ted was gone, killed while flying over the angry skies of Vietnam. He was one of many who would not be coming home. I cried for him then, I cried when I touched his name on the Vietnam Wall, and I still cry even as I write these words.

Most deaths in Vietnam were just statistics to me. We learned, no matter what happened, just to keep going. I even kept going when they loaded dead American bodies onto my plane to begin their long and final journey home. I kept going even when I discovered one of those bodies had been a member of my own squadron.

It was hard for me, however, to keep going when Ted died. He'd been more than a friend; he had been "closer than a brother." Still, I had young pilots to train who were depending upon me. I *had* to keep going if they were going to have a chance.

While Ted never came home to the US, as a fellow believer, he did go home. That is the comfort I take when I consider his early death. There is a day coming when together we will catch up on our lives. And, together, we will finally see and touch the face of God.

High Flight

Oh, I have slipped the surly bonds of earth
And danced the skies on laughter-silvered wings;
Sunward I've climbed, and joined the tumbling mirth
Of sun-split clouds . . . and done a hundred things
You have not dreamed of . . . wheeled and soared and swung
High in the sunlit silence. Hov'ring there,
I've chased the shouting wind along, and flung
My eager craft through footless halls of air.
Up, up the long, delirious, burning blue
I've topped the windswept heights with easy grace
Where never lark, or even eagle flew.
And, while with silent, lifting mind I've trod
The high untresspassed sanctity of space
Put out my hand, and touched the face of God.

—John Gillespie Magee, Jr.[7]

URBAN FIRE

★

He shall cover you with His feathers, and under His wings
shall you take refuge; His truth shall be your shield and buckler.
You shall not be afraid of the terror by night, nor of the
arrow that flies by day (Ps. 91: 4-5).

I can't remember whether I heard the blast or felt it first. I had been walking with a fellow peacekeeper in the heart of Ben Yehuda's outdoor shopping mall. Jerusalem was usually crowded with tourists in June but it was mid-afternoon and the shopping crowds had thinned. An explosion erupted in front of me and a blast of hot air swept past me as I turned and fell to my knees. It was my second day on the job.

I had always dreamed of going to Israel. As the cradle of the Christian faith, it held a certain special quality that drew me to it. I dreamed of walking where Jesus once walked and seeing what He saw. So when the call came notifying me that I was being assigned to the Middle East I was excited.

The month before departing for my new tour of duty, we received the shocking news that the senior American officer in Israel had just been murdered. He had been on patrol in southern Lebanon when he was taken prisoner. His captivity ended in a brutal death. The world I was headed to was clearly far different from the open plains of the Midwest.

Upon landing at Ben Gurion airport, my driver briefed me on the current state of affairs in the city. Things were stable, but unrest from Gaza had spread into Jerusalem. He advised me to be watchful, vary my route to and from the headquarters, and maintain a very low profile. This was standard anti-terrorism procedure.

The first day was filled with a long series of indoctrination briefings. I was thrilled to learn the second day would be free for us to take in the city. Early the next morning I left the American Colony Hotel and headed out toward the Old City.

I was walking through an outdoor shopping mall when a nearby building exploded into the crowd. The blast rained dust and debris for 100 yards, knocking people to the ground. Dazed, I choked back the dust, got up from the ground, and staggered away from the rubble. My ears rang and my eyes burned, but I was alive and wanted to stay that way. I'd had enough of the city, but I couldn't escape. The crowds in front of me seemed to be growing, and there was angry shouting as armed soldiers began to stream past. Two kids tossed molotov cocktails that shattered when they landed inside parked cars. Smoke poured from the cars, and then flames could be seen. I tried to exit the area by moving in a new direction toward King Herod's gate. Cars were passing, and a jeep carrying soldiers was speeding down the street when an elderly woman found herself in their path. The jeep hit her and she flew into a group of men standing nearby.

The jeep stopped but the soldiers remained inside. An angry crowd began to gather around the jeep and were shaking it and screaming. Trapped in the middle of a growing mass of people, and unable to understand what they were saying, I looked over at the elderly woman on the ground. Either she was dead or unconscious, I couldn't tell. Then I was pushed by the crowd away from where she lay. Everything was chaos. Suddenly, there was another loud explosion in the street. Someone had tossed an explosive device at the jeep. I saw people around me with blood on their clothes and their faces.

My head hurt, I felt dizzy, and all I could think was, *Lord have mercy; Lord protect me!* I turned in the direction of the hotel and pushed against the crowds. And then I was surprised to see an opening appear in front of me. I forced my way through it and up a hill away from the chaos.

As I reached the top of the hill, the smoke cleared and my eyes stopped burning. I turned and looked back at the ancient walls and the angry crowds in the distance. Watching the bedlam, I wondered if peace were truly possible in such a divided city. A moment passed and I decided it wasn't wise to remain any longer. Brushing myself off, I swallowed hard and gave thanks to God who had kept me safe three times in the last hour.

A Time
to Laugh

Against the assault of laughter,
nothing can stand.
Mark Twain

His laughter sparkled like a
splash of water in sunlight.
Joseph Lelyveld

He who laughs, lasts.
Mary Pettibone Poole

RENT-A YENTA

★

ELLIE KAY
USAF MILITARY WIFE

She girds herself with strength, And makes her arms strong. . .
Strength and dignity are her clothing, And she smiles at the future
(Prov. 31:17, 25 NAS).

My husband was flying an F-117 stealth fighter jet somewhere over the Middle East during the last days of Desert Storm. I was back home managing a storm of my own: a three year old, an eighteen month old, and a newborn. To win the war I would battle this morning, I knew I had to have my troops up by sunrise—for I'd discovered the best time to attack the grocery store was by dawn's early light.

If you have never been to the grocery store before 7:00 A.M., I recommend it. Meeting interesting characters (the kind who are out shopping before sane people have had their first sip of coffee) makes it worth the extra effort.

On this morning, I drove to the store and stuffed my three kids in the cart. I pulled my basket of kids-on-wheels toward the checkout, pushing another cart full of groceries at the same time. This was no easy operation, but with a husband on deployment it was my only option.

As I rounded the corner near an Oreo™ cookie display, I nearly ran over a Yenta. Yes, Yenta. As in "little Jewish matchmaker," the one from *Fiddler on the Roof.* She was diminutive—two inches shy of five feet—but her expression was imposing enough to make up for what she lacked in inches. She wore her gray hair wrapped in a scarf and, in spite of her thick New York accent, she even sounded like Yenta.

"Oh my goodness, oh my gosh!" the woman exclaimed, smacking her forehead with her open palm. "I can't believe what I see heyah." She pointed at me, "Can you believe this?"

Yenta squinted her eyes in deep concern, patting my arm as she spoke. "Did you knowah? Did you knowah, that you could put yah back out doing that?"

Way down the aisle, she spied a stock boy unloading boxes in the dairy section. Not a problem for Yenta. She stood on her toes and shouted, "Hey youwah! Yeah, you mista! I don't mean ya' mutha', I don't mean ya' fatha', I mean YOUWAH! COME HEAYAH NOW!"

The startled stock boy came running as she scolded him. "Did yah know that this woman is going to put her back out?" She stomped her foot. "Yes, she's going to put her back out and where will ya' be then, I ASK YOU? You'll be in the poorhouse, that's what. She'll put her back out, sue your store, and you'll be out of a job, that's what. So ya'd bettah push her cart to the check out and ya'd bettah do it NOW!"

Not wanting to lose his job or take on a lawsuit, the boy immediately went to work pushing my cart of groceries. Overwhelmed by the entire experience, I stared at Yenta and just smiled.

Some days it seems that I'm clothed with exhaustion and peanut butter stains rather than strength and dignity, as the Book of Proverbs suggests. But Proverbs also says, "she smiles at the future." I've made an amazing discovery. Smiling at the future (or the present) creates a beautiful garment of strength. There is a time to laugh, and finding humor in challenging situations has given me the strength to be an overcomer. Especially on those days when I'm clothed with exhaustion and peanut butter stains rather than strength and dignity.

Yenta saw me staring at her and confided, "I know what yah thinking. Yes, I know what yah thinking."

She struck the pose of a saint, one hand gently resting in the palm of the other. "You're thinking that ya'd like to say thank you. No need to say thanks, I do things like this because I love people. A poor widow woman all alone in the world, but I'm always thinking of others. Yes, I love people, that's what."

In her own way, Yenta loved me that day, though I couldn't help but be a little embarrassed by all the commotion. But come to think of it, I could use a little help like that once in a while. Now if I could just remember where I put her phone number. . . .

(Used with permission of author Ellie Kay, abridged from *Shop Save and Share*.)

BLUE-JEANED STEALTH QUEEN

★

ELLIE KAY
USAF WIFE

Before destruction the heart of a man is haughty,
And before honor is humility (Prov. 18:12).

Humility? Horse feathers! I don't need to learn humility. After all, I'm not an *overly* proud person. Sure, I'm pleased with the fact that I lost *almost* all my added weight after having five babies in the first seven years of marriage. Add the fact that our military family has moved eleven times in thirteen years and you'll see why I'm *proud* that I still have my sanity. But that's not spiritual *pride*, it is satisfaction over great achievement—right?

Oh, it's true that someone once told me that I was too proud of my whole wheat honey nut bread—but how many women do you know who grind their own wheat berries and add rice and millet to complete the protein? Is it *wrong* to want to put Martha Stewart to shame? Is that pride? I don't think so. I'm *not* the kind of haughty person that Proverbs is talking about. In fact, I've always taken great *pride* in my sense of *humility*. Uh, oh, I think I'm about to get another lesson on the "h" word.

Just about the time I convince myself I've got a grip on these issues, God shines His spotlight and shows me I still need work. If it's true that humility comes before great honor, then God must have something incredible in store for me. I seem to regularly go through the humbling process. Last month I was given a strong dose of humility during a photo shoot at my husband's Stealth Fighter Squadron in a place called "The Canyon."

Every year, the unit brings out a dozen sleek, black F-117 stealth fighters onto the flight line ramp for us. We were instructed to wear white t-shirts, brown bomber jackets (borrowed from our hubbies), and blue jeans with black boots. We dubbed ourselves the blue-jeaned stealth queens as we strutted our stuff in front of the jets. Never mind the fact that all together we had 48 kids, 187 loads of laundry, and 37 dogs waiting for us at home. We were proud that we still had "it." The only problem was—most of us couldn't remember where we put it.

Instead of the mandatory white t-shirt, I had an ecru colored shirt on. I thought the jacket would cover it and no one would notice. I was wrong.

When we were ready to walk out with the photographer, a mean-eyed mama thrust a white t-shirt under my nose and hissed, "Quick, put this on, that ecru colored shirt will ruin the overall effect." These blue-jeaned baby queens are serious about their photo ops.

Now is a good time to mention an important fact about a certain disability I have. You see, when God passed out the common sense, he gave my friend Myra a double portion and reduced my part to a morsel.

So, I stood there, looking at the guys on the flight line. The entire crew was resting in the shade by the jets. There were no bathrooms nearby, and the mean-eyed mama was staring at me with her lips tensed, tapping her foot. I didn't have time to run back to the main buildings to change. How in the world was I going to take off my ecru shirt and change into the white t-shirt in front of God and country and mechanics? I might be strutting my stuff, but my pride didn't want everyone to *see* my stuff.

A tap on the shoulder interrupted my thoughts. It was common sense Myra.

"Ellie, you could just slip the white t-shirt right *over* the shirt you're wearing now" she said.

"Uh, yes, uh, of course," I stammered wondering why I hadn't thought of the obvious.

I quickly pulled on the white t-shirt and then found myself faced with a yet another problem. You see, when a woman has had a basketball team's worth of children and when this said woman really loves coffee and chocolate, there's a basic problem. I was wearing

"Great Shapes" pantyhose (guaranteed to take five pounds off any figure). I was wearing two pair to remove that extra ten pounds.

There was no way I could leave that shirt untucked or the added bulk would make me look like a buffalo in that canyon. It wasn't just a matter of pride. I had the image of all the wives in the photo to consider.

Once again, my hero, Myra, saw this dilemma and said, "Here, Ellie, Marcia and I will hold up our jackets while you tuck your shirt in."

What a relief!

The two women held up their jackets, shielding the view from the flight-crew members by the jets.

Quickly, I dropped my pants, neatly tucked in my shirt (removing at least five pounds of bulk) and pulled them up again. With a sigh of relief, I zipped the jeans and turned around to pick up my jacket from the pavement. At that moment, I got my dose of God-given humility.

To my utter embarrassment, I noticed for the first time, a row of twelve other men sitting in the shade of the hangar about 200 yards behind me. The women shielded the view of the guys in front of us, however, no one noticed the group behind us. There wasn't an improvised jacket curtain for that crowd.

Myra noticed the Peeping Toms at the same time I did and was quick to comfort me with, "Hey, Ellie, don't worry about it. I don't think they even noticed, there's so much going on."

Momentary relief accompanied my hope that maybe Myra was right and they hadn't noticed. Still, I had to confirm Myra's assessment, so I slowly stole a side-glance at the group sitting in the shade.

They were looking at me, slapping each other on the back—and laughing. Laughing hysterically, laughing like lunatics, laughing enough to turn my face beet-red.

Yep, I'm proud of my humility. And, oh by the way, Lord, anytime You want to move on to a different lesson—that's okay by me.

(Used with permission of author Ellie Kay, abridged from *Shop Save and Share*.)

"CHEEL OUT, MON"

★

A soft answer turns away wrath,
But a harsh word stirs up anger (Prov. 15:1).

I've been in the Air Force for over twenty years and have worked with officers from all services. In that time, I've never yet met an unfit marine. Some of the sharpest looking, sharpest talking officers I've worked with have been marine officers. But the attitude they bring of being ready to "rock and roll" in battle can create conflict in other situations. One of those occurred while I held a military/diplomatic position in Egypt near the end of the Cold War.

I was serving as a military observer in the Middle East ensuring that the various sides of the Camp David agreement fulfilled their promises. All services were represented as well as military members from nineteen different nations, including China and the Soviet Union.

In addition to verifying treaty compliance we participated in a number of embassy functions in Cairo. Each of the nineteen nations had one day a year where it hosted a major party to celebrate its "national day." For the US, the obvious date was July 4th, and it was customary to try to outdo the other nations. The US celebration party started at noon on Saturday and didn't end until late Sunday afternoon.

When the day came for the Soviets to celebrate, they were in the mood to outdo what the US had done the summer before. Their party took place on October 17th as a way of remembering the Bolshevik Revolution in the early part of the twentieth century.

The evening was clear and crisp, and several hundred formally dressed dignitaries arrived to celebrate with the Soviets. My wife, Cindy, and I were impressed from the moment we walked in. Cindy moved off to greet the Soviet wives, and I to meet the Soviet officers.

At the time, there was tremendous distrust between the US and Soviet Union that extended down to the troop level. Even the Soviet wives were taught not to trust those from the "decadent west."

Cindy sat at a table with seven Soviet women. Since we were soon to be reassigned back home, one wife asked Cindy, "So, I suppose you'll be sorry to be going home soon?" My wife was surprised by the question, and asked, "Why do you say that?" She answered emphatically, "Well, you're going to miss the wonderful shopping here in Cairo—all the food they have in their stores is so wonderful!"

Now, you've got to understand that the major grocery store we all shopped at in Cairo was the size of a 7 Eleven. Cindy replied, "No, actually our stores in the United States are five to ten times as large as the stores here."

The women looked around at each other with obvious surprise on their faces. Then a knowing look came over them. The woman sitting next to Cindy nodded her head, patted Cindy on the arm, and said compassionately, "Of course they are, dear."

Those women were certain Cindy had given the required political answer. They didn't believe her for a minute, but understood the dilemma she was in. A political officer told them how to answer such questions and kept them in line. They assumed Cindy had the same kind of guidance.

There was a table of marine officers in their best formal uniforms seated next to a group of Soviet officers. The vodka had been flowing freely for some time when the Soviet political officer, Major Valentin, began to make disparaging remarks about the bourgeois lifestyle of Americans.

He shot loaded questions across the tables like "If a democracy is such a great thing, why did you have slaves? We never had to enslave part of our people to make our nation great!" The marines gritted their teeth and held their tongues. "If you're supposed to be in favor of freedom, why does your country have the greatest number of prisoners of any nation on earth?" He smiled venomously as he downed another glass of vodka. That did it. The marines began to toss taunts like hand grenades back across the table. This didn't help, because, along with the vodka, it only fueled his fire.

"At least in communism we don't have poor living in ghettos, without enough food to feed their families." He took another drink of vodka and spat out, "If you believed everyone is equal why did you put all the Japanese in concentration camps in WWII?" The marines stood up and were about to storm the beaches to pound this rather small, but loud, Soviet major.

Something had to be done quick, so I yelled, "Hey, Valentin!" He turned with a silly grin on his face and looked at me. "Hey, I want to teach you a famous American slogan." He looked a little surprised. "Yeah? What is this famous American slogan?"

"Whenever someone gets too worked up and excited we say this. It is very useful."

"Well, tell me what this is."

"It is very special, Valentin, and very American."

"So tell me! What is it?"

"We say, 'Chill out, man,' but it's pronounced correctly this way; 'Cheel out, mon.'"

He smiled and tried to repeat it. "Chel out, men."

"No Valentin, you pronounce it, 'Cheel out, mon.'" It took another try and he had it. He smiled triumphantly at the marines in front of him. Then he turned to his fellow Soviet officers and mimicked the accent perfectly, "Cheel out, mon." The Marines at the table next to him burst out laughing. They kept rolling till they almost fell out of their seats. Valentin looked at them thinking they were laughing at him. But they cheered him on.

"That's right Valentin. You've got it. Say it again."

From that moment on, he was on a one-man mission. He wandered from table to table telling almost anyone who was talking, "Cheel out, mon!"

The atmosphere completely changed. Valentin thought he was really great because he had learned an American colloquialism, and the marines were entertained rather than infuriated.

Looking back on that night, it seems a bit silly now. But the alternative could have created an embarrassing incident that would have further angered both sides. A soft answer can truly turn away anger. I learned humor can often do the same thing.

PILOTS NEVER PANIC

★

ELLIE KAY
USAF WIFE

As I was with Moses, so I will be with you.
I will not leave you nor forsake you (Josh. 1:5).

I'm not the first military wife to have a baby without her husband at her side. Even though I'm not a betting woman, I will say that chances are good I won't be the last. At least my husband, Bob, wasn't deployed or flying in harm's way. But whether he's there or not, one thing remains constant—God will always be with me. He proved that to me in a special way, one early winter morning.

"K-Bob, hasn't your wife pickled yet?" laughed Moose as he sat at the operations desk of the flying squadron next to another pilot called Stinky.

K-Bob shook his head, "No, but if she calls, you'd better come and get me *right away*, the doctor says this one won't take long since it's our fifth. She's already doing that 'facing stuff.'" With that, he left the room and went to get his helmet for the next flight.

Moose chuckled and whispered to Stinky, "I got ten bucks that says she goes so fast that old K-Bob misses the birth!"

"Are you kidding?" Stinky replied, "K-Bob is ready to jump at a moment's notice. He's been so edgy it's hard to get him to fly."

Stinky scratched his head as he continued, "You know it's tough when a pilot like K-Bob hates to fly the early go, worrying about his wife pickling while he's up in the air. I say he makes it—I'll take that bet."

7:00 a.m. At another part of the base.

I woke up to get the children ready for an 8:00 departure for a doctor's appointment. Since I was three weeks past due, I had to fill out paperwork to have labor induced. I'd already arranged for childcare with my friend Beth. I was having a few mild contractions, but I figured they were just like the false labor pains I'd had for the last two months.

7:30 a.m.

My friend Pauline called from Colorado and I told her of my discouragement at having to be induced. (I'd had all my other children with no drugs or IVs—in the hospital, but all natural.) I asked her to pray that these contractions would get stronger and turn into the real thing on their own.

7:33 a.m. and 7:36 a.m.

I hung up the phone and the first hard contraction hit, followed by another strong one *three* minutes later. I remember thinking, "Wow! When Pauline prays things happen!"

7:38 a.m.

The third contraction hit at two minutes and I had a hard one followed by two milder ones. Then the strangest thing happened—I felt the need to drive myself to pick up Bob rather than call someone to get me.

7:39 a.m.

The PA system blared the announcement, "Hey K-Bob, your flight is moving out, you need to stuff your parachute and get out there with them." Moose turned to Stinky, "You know a guy has got it bad when you have to remind him it's time to step to the airplane."

7:40 a.m.

My son Daniel helped his younger siblings get into the van and I drove them to Beth's house. I arrived at the curb with the horn blaring.

She ran out of her house as I yelled, "I'm in labor and I'm going to go pick up Bob!"

Beth grabbed fourteen-month-old Jonathan out of his car seat, "Don't you think I should drive you, Ellie?"

I put the van into gear, "No! I'm going to get Bob—don't call him or he'll panic. He's cagey enough as it is!"

7:44 a.m.

"Hey K-Bob, waddaya doin' looking out that window at the parking lot? Daydreaming?" Stinky shook his head as he gave Moose a knowing look.

"No, I was just thinking. . . ." K-Bob's sentence was interrupted as he saw a familiar blue van pull into the parking lot. "Hey, that's Ellie. I wonder what's she's doing here. Maybe she baked bread again this morning."

At the sound of food, Moose's eyes lit up, "Yea, I love it when she brings it in straight from the oven." His mouth began to water.

7:45 a.m.

He met my van outside and stuck his head in the open car window, "Hi, Beloved, are you dropping off some bread for the guys?"

I put the van in park, "Yeah, honey, I'm dropping something—but it ain't bread!"

I was in between contractions, "This is it, I'm in labor!" I announced.

Even though he's had *many* children, Bob has panicked every time I had a baby. He stood there in his flight suit just staring blank-faced at me.

I repeated, "Come on, let's go!"

He turned pale. "Are you kidding?"

I felt another *hard* contraction coming. "No, let's go NOW!"

Bob ran back into the squadron while I slowly moved to the passenger side of the van.

7:46 a.m.

In the squadron, Bob dropped his parachute on the floor and shouted to Moose and Stinky, "I'm having a baby!" Then he dashed out of the squadron and jumped into the van.

Stinky turned to Moose and smiled confidently, "Looks like you're going to owe me some money, dude."

Always up for a challenge, Moose retorted, "She hasn't pickled yet, we'll see!"

7:47 a.m.

As Bob took the steering wheel to drive to the hospital I concentrated on my breathing. The contractions were now one minute apart and very intense. Bob panicked as usual and drove like a nuclear scramble alert to get to the hospital.

We stopped at a red light and in between contractions I issued reminders. "Beloved, please get the video camera out of the van and don't forget my bag, either."

As the light turned green, he took off faster than any dragster on the block and declared, "The contractions are less than a minute apart! Don't worry about the camera! Just concentrate on your breathing!"

7:59 A.M.

Our van screamed into the hospital parking lot as Bob pulled into a "no parking" slot in front of the ER doors. With the van engine running, Bob dashed into the emergency room and shouted, "My wife is having a baby, NOW!"

The staff looked up at the crazed father-to-be in a flight suit. Bob allowed them exactly *two seconds* to move and then grabbed a wheelchair, slammed it through the ER doors and brought it outside, where I was standing by the van.

He helped me into the chair mumbling, "We've got a bunch of rocket scientists in there."

Once inside, he ran down the hall, ramming me into an occasional wall when he turned a tight corner. I couldn't talk because my contractions were only a few seconds apart. Even though I couldn't speak, my mind was saying, *Bob, I am in labor here. Would you please stop using me as a missile?!*

8:01 a.m.

Just then I saw the double doors to Labor and Delivery at the end of a long hall. I was relieved we were almost there. My relief rapidly turned into concern because the wheelchair was not *losing* speed, it was *gaining* momentum as Bob sought to accomplish his mission.

My mind shouted, *The door! The door! It's an automatic door with a button on the side of the wall! It's not designed to be opened by the feet of women in wheelchairs! You'd better slow down or this is the last child you'll ever have!*

Bob slammed the chair through the double doors, much to the surprise of the nursing staff at the nearby desk. I heard him mumble, "Some automatic doors!"

8:03 a.m.

The nurses were shocked at our ill-mannered arrival.

"Wait a minute! Who are you?" They asked the overzealous pilot and his human battering ram.

"I'm Bob, and *she*," he pointed to me, "is going to *have* that baby right now!" His eyes were wild as he tried to convince the veteran nurses of my advanced condition.

I couldn't respond because I was focusing on a screw in the door hinge as I breathed my way through another intense contraction.

Apparently, Bob thought the nurses were hearing impaired because he kept shouting answers to their questions with high-pitched responses such as:

"Ellie Kay!"

"Forty-three weeks!"

"Fifth child!"

"Dr. Holzhauer!"

"Of course I'm the father! Who else do you think the father is? What are you? A rocket scientist?"

Then, as a drowning man will come up one more time for air, he bellowed, "Oh, my goodness, the van engine is still running and it's parked in the ER zone!"

Then . . . he was gone.

8:05 a.m.

With the Red Baron out of the room, the nurses relaxed as they gave me a robe and helped me to the bathroom to change. No sooner had I got the robe on than the baby slammed down the birth canal.

I held onto the metal rail for support and called to the nurses, "Whoa! Something's happening here, I need your help!"

The nurses helped me to the bed and I lay back on the pillows exclaiming again, "Something's happening!"

The nurse took one look and said, "Lady, you're about to have a baby!"

The meaning of her words sunk in as she shouted, "She's complete! Emergency delivery! Labor room two! Get Dr. Holzhauer—STAT!"

The other nurse asked, "Where's her husband?"

I answered in my mind, *He's parking the car!*

Thankfully, the doctor was in the hospital making rounds and arrived in seconds, out of breath from running. He kneeled by my side and whispered, "Whenever you're ready, Ellie, I'm right here."

8:08 a.m.

Exactly three minutes after arriving in the labor and delivery room, Joshua Steven was born weighing ten pounds and bellowing like a fighter pilot.

About that time, Bob raced back in the room shouting, "How is she?"

"Mistah" said an old, Southern nurse, "You done had yourself a fine man-child!"

He looked to the warming tray and saw his son, a virtual Baby Huey. Joshua earned the nickname Conan the Baby Barbarian because he always did things in a big way. He was delivered just twenty-eight minutes after I picked Bob up from work.

"A baby!" Bob yelled, "I was just parking the car!"

8:15 a.m.

The phone rang and Moose picked it up, "49FTS, can I help you?"

He paused, "What? It's only been half an hour since you left here, she's pickled already?"

Stinky whispered, "I told you I'd win!"

Suddenly Moose smiled broadly, and trying to stay sympathetic he said, "Oh, gee, that's too bad."

He hung up the phone and stuck out his hand with a smirk on his face, "Pay up, Stinky. The poor guy missed the whole thing while he was parking the car."

Unlike us, God never misses anything. He sees the parade from the beginning to the end. He knows where you are and what you need, and he'll be by your side when you need him—even if your husband is parking the car.

(Used with permission of author Ellie Kay, abridged from *How to Save Money Every Day*.)

A WEE BIT OF IRISH

★

I will bless the Lord at all times;
His praise shall continually be in my mouth. Psalm 34:1

When I was in high school, I never realized my involvement in acting might actually save my life. But it wasn't until I finished a particularly dangerous tour of duty in the Middle East that I had my drama final exam.

In 1991, just before coalition forces launched their combined assault on Iraq to free Kuwait, we faced a growing threat from terrorism. As a UN peacekeeper, a westerner in the Middle East, I was viewed by many as an "infidel," polluting the very ground I walked on. At the time my duty was to patrol, in a UN vehicle, a fairly remote desert location along with officers from nineteen different nations.

As the tensions grew, it became more and more apparent that Americans needed to maintain an even lower profile. In the streets of Cairo, we stopped wearing our standard battle dress fatigues with American flags on the side. A more generic shirt was deemed safer, but even this wouldn't prove enough on a sunny day in October.

Patrolling alone wasn't a particularly taxing assignment. I just didn't like being alone in the desert. I would have preferred the company of another to pass the hours in the sun and lean on if I ran into trouble. Yet we were short manned and there were more chances of getting lost in the desert than running into unfriendly elements. I used a compass and map and some well-known landmarks to navigate the terrain. Moving out early one morning, I had been on the road about an hour when I approached a Bedouin walking in the sand. It's the custom in the desert to pick up those walking and he got into the front seat with me.

What always surprised me in these situations was how the Bedouins knew where they were in an unmarked and shifting terrain. About twenty minutes later the Bedouin signaled he wanted out, and I stopped the vehicle. He waved good-bye and headed off in another direction. Again, there were no landmarks, he just knew. I was smiling as I came up over the next ridge when my heart stopped.

There in the road were three men wearing checkered scarves over their faces holding automatic weapons. As they saw me, they aimed their barrels at the front of my vehicle. Now a Jeep is a pretty tough vehicle, but a 7.62mm round will penetrate the engine and come out the other side. There was no way out of this situation— only a quick prayer to the Lord and they were upon me.

"American? American?"

"Sure and t'isn't it a fine day. My wee family and I are from County Cork, Ireland. A fine place it 'tis," I replied in my best Irish brogue.

They looked into the back of the vehicle for other passengers.

"American? Are you American?"

"Now lad, do I luke like an American? Aye, they're a crusty lot. What brings you boys out this early in the morning?"

They looked at me and then at each other and then they waved their guns at me signaling me to move on. I slowly depressed the accelerator and moved forward. My heart began to beat rapidly as I saw them scatter and move off into the desert.

I stopped a few miles down the road, got out of the vehicle and took a number of deep breaths. Running over those few seconds again in my mind, it seemed surreal. A minute at the most and I was on my way. What could I possibly report on? A chance encounter in a desert wasteland. I never saw their faces and couldn't have identified them if I had to. Yet, the outcome could have been . . . who knows?

The Lord promised we would have the words of testimony in the hour we needed them. Now I didn't give much of a testimony there, and I don't know what my old drama teacher would have thought. I got a C from him in high school. But after that, I never felt alone. I knew an unseen companion was seated right beside me.

A TIME FOR HEROES (PART 1)

★

THE HANOI HILTON⁸
CAPTAIN EUGENE "RED" MCDANIEL
USN (RETIRED)

For He Himself has said,
"I will never leave you nor forsake you" (Heb. 13:5).

I was awakened from sleep by a call from the duty officer notifying me of our upcoming mission. It would be a maximum effort "alpha strike" against the strategic truck repair center and marshaling yards at Van Dien, south of Hanoi. We referred to it as "Little Detroit." The strike would take us through "white knuckle alley" and heavy concentrations of anti-aircraft flak and surface-to-air missiles. We all knew that clusters of batteries, capable of peppering the sky with flak bursts and radar-guided SAM missiles, surrounded Van Dien.

After reviewing weather reports and surveying photographs of the target area, we finished our briefing and headed topside for our standard litany of pre-flight instrument checks. Kelly Patterson would be my bombardier-navigator for that morning mission in 1967. Checkout complete, I felt the sudden shock of the catapult hurling our A-6 Intruder off the pitching flight deck of the *Enterprise*. We were loaded with 13,000 pounds of ordnance.

In a few minutes, we rendezvoused overhead with the rest of the squadron, then headed toward the North Vietnamese coast. Our formation penetrated North Vietnamese airspace at 15,000 feet through a broken layer of sky blue and patchy white clouds. We had flown about 60 miles inland when we started seeing SAM missiles rising up in front of us. They looked like a barrage of telephone poles that had been flung skyward. I was starting evasive maneuvers when the red light on my ECM (Electronic Countermeasures) started flashing. The ominous warbling, "whoooo, whoooo, whoooo . . ." echoed through my headset, warning us that a ground radar and SAM battery had locked on and were tracking us. We were twenty-five seconds into evasive dodging when a violent explosion jarred the aircraft, sending us into a dive. Red lights on the console indicated a fire in the port engine, hydraulic systems were out, the control stick was frozen, and we were dropping fast. We had to get out before our bomb load blew.

My visual display indicator, which showed my flight path in relation to the ground, indicated that we were sliding off and down to the right. The altimeter gauge was spinning backwards as we descended toward a jungle mountain range in the distance. We were riding down a burning jet whose speed had reached nearly 550 knots. You were not supposed to eject at over 500 knots because the canopy could jam. I asked Kelly, "How about it? Do you want to try for the mountain?" Kelly gave the affirmative. We both knew from navy survival training that riding our aircraft to an uninhabited area gave RESCAP (Rescue Combat Air Patrol) the greatest chance of getting to us before the Viet Cong.

At about 2,000 feet above the approaching range, I yelled at Kelly, "Let's get out!" The canopy blew amid a blast of high velocity turbulence and cockpit debris. Kelly shot out first and I followed into a confused somersault before the violent jerk of shroud lines and the billowing parachute slowed my descent. I felt like a puppet on strings dangling over enemy territory. As I floated down, I could see Kelly's chute far off to the right and the pall of black smoke where our A-6 had plowed into the mountain.

The parachute had slowed my free-fall, but due to jagged rips in the chute, I was descending dangerously fast. All I could do was hang on helplessly and watch the jungle rush up toward me. In moments, I crashed through layers of canopy until an abrupt halt left me dangling fifty feet above the jungle floor, snagged on one of the branches. There I was, 10,000 miles from home, stranded in the middle of North Vietnam, gently swaying from a tree while the enemy closed in.

I knew I couldn't just hang there and do nothing. I had a better chance committing myself to a hostile jungle than waiting to be taken prisoner. The only obstacle was getting down. I started crawling up the risers of my chute when the sickening sound of ripping nylon sent me slamming into the jungle floor with such an impact that two of my vertebrae were crushed in the fall.

"Red, are you okay? It was Nick Carpenter, my back-up man, calling me on the radio. I reached into my vest and pulled out my small survival radio. "I'm okay, Nick. My back's pretty bad, but I'm okay." I looked up through the holes in the canopy and saw Nick's A-6 circling protectively overhead, then he veered off toward the coast. Still, I was thankful to God that Nick had pinpointed my location. I wasn't stranded. I knew RESCAP, which had a reputation for its uncanny ability to pluck pilots from hostile territory, would soon be on the way with a Jolly Green Giant rescue helicopter. I found myself praying, "And thank you, God, Dorothy will know I'm on the ground okay."

While waiting, I buried my chute, strapped on my survival kit, and started climbing up the lush jungle incline, pausing every so often to listen to whistles of the Vietnamese search parties combing the jungle in pursuit. I tried to make contact with Kelly over the radio, but there was no response. As the darkness squeezed the last rays out of the brooding jungle, I fell into an uncomfortable sleep—waiting for my deliverance.

I passed apprehensive hours listening to the night sounds of the jungle, but nothing. The claustrophobic darkness was slowly choking out my hopes for a rescue. I began to pray from a position of urgency that I had never confronted before. "Please, God, get me out of this." I was asking for a miracle. "Please, God, lift me out of this jungle and back to the deck of *Enterprise*." But more hours passed, broken only by the infrequent screech of a bird, the chattering of monkeys, and the snapping of twigs high in the overhead canopy. I strained to hear the distant drone of planes, but nothing. I reminded God in the darkness that I was a good Baptist, a deacon in my church, a believer in Him. I thought about my family—Dorothy, Mike, David, and my baby daughter, Leslie. How would they take the news of my shoot-down? And I found myself asking, "Why me, God? Why me?"

Dawn came around 5:30, but still no planes. I moved back down the slope to where I had buried the parachute to unfurl it on the ground as a marking signal, even though I knew it would expose my position to the VC search parties as well. It was calculated risk I had to take. Moments later, I heard an A-6 overhead, accompanied by an F-4 fighter escort. I radioed them and was told to hold tight. A Jolly Green Giant helicopter would be coming in forty-five minutes to pick me up. "Outstanding!" I shouted back. My emotions soared. But minutes dragged by, then several hours, with no chopper in sight. About one o'clock, I heard the lone crack of a rifle and felt a sudden surge of adrenaline. I turned around, and all my hopes came crashing down. In moments, fifteen jabbering Vietnamese peasants had surrounded me. There was no escape.

After trussing my arms behind my back, they led me through the jungle until we reached a small hamlet where I was strip searched and left bound in a small room, waiting for the next move. Besides the nagging pain in my back, my arms and legs were swollen and numb from the tight ropes. After an hour, I was given back my flight suit and began an agonizing journey by foot and truck to Hanoi. It was a painful trip through a gauntlet of rifle butts, taunts, leg kicking, face slapping, and the galling humiliation of feeling like a captured animal. The closer we got to Hanoi, the rougher the treatment got. Sadistic specters of torture pricked my mind as we neared our destination—specters that would assume a ruthless reality in the years ahead.

I finally arrived at the Hanoi Hilton, the main American prison camp, on a Sunday morning. My introduction to North Vietnamese interrogation began shortly after my arrival. To extract information they tied my wrists, then pulled my arms high behind me so that my shoulder bones were ready to pop. It was a procedure I would become intimately acquainted with during my six years of confinement. My body was contorted into a position it wasn't designed to adjust to. The pain was excruciating. My numbed brain struggled to compute what they wanted: Military information? A confession?

Every man possesses a different breaking point beyond which

there is no endurance. I didn't know where mine was, but I was determined not to give in to their interrogating and political hammering. I would die first. Name, rank, serial number—that was all. All I could do was pray, "Please, God, give me strength to resist, to go out with some kind of dignity." After three days of relentless interrogation, the brutality had not budged me, so they gave up and threw me into an isolation cell clamped in leg irons.

In my musty, gray, solitary cell, reality finally hit. I was a prisoner of war, facing an indefinite sentence. While preparing for eighty-one combat missions over the north, I had considered the possibility that I might be killed. To die suddenly was one thing. It was easier reconciling myself to that potential than to be captured. I wasn't prepared for that.

I knew it would be a long war, and I knew I had to resist. I had to find a way to resist. I couldn't let myself rot in resignation. I had to keep fighting. It was going to demand everything within me and then some. I knew there were other American prisoners facing the same grim future and fearing the worst. I could tell by their screams that more was in store for me. We were up against an enemy who found pleasure in inflicting pain. I knew I had to establish communication with the other Americans to bolster our morale, rally our resolve, and give and take moral support for the long haul ahead. If we wanted to keep our sanity, we had to stick together.

Yet, I also knew that I had to lay hold of God more than I had ever done in the past. I knew my strength would soon run out. I had to lay hold of a stronger Rock.

Just then, the jiggling sound of the jailer's key brought me out of my reflections. The dreaded metallic rattling sound would become a familiar, hated noise in the days and years ahead. It was always a portent of impending pain.

The guard unshackled the leg irons and jerked me to my feet. I was pushed down the dingy corridor, dragging my half-limp leg, before being shoved into another gray cell. In the dimness, I focused on eyes shining from hollow sockets. It was another flyer grinning at me. He was lying on the concrete floor, naked, with an ugly laceration running twelve inches from his wrist to his elbow. He had a gaping hole in his left leg, caked reddish brown with blood; the other leg was broken.

When I saw young Bill Metzger lying there grinning up at me, I stopped feeling so sorry for myself. I stopped asking "Why me, God?" and wondered "Why not me?" I remembered the times I had sat in the comfort of my padded pew on Sunday mornings back home and agreed with the words of the Apostle Paul: "And we know that all things work together for good to those who love God, to those who are the called according to His purpose." (Rom. 8:28) It was so easy in the sanctuary of America to nod a casual assent to that great assurance. But now, the severe confines of a military prison forced me to contemplate the force of that promise in a way I had never done before.

"If that verse it true, " I said to myself, "if any of what I call my faith is true, then that verse applies here in Hanoi, right in this cell. If, in God's scheme of things, there's a purpose for my being here, I can make it—even as a wretched prisoner caged like an animal, starved, beaten, and brutalized. God, if I can muster what little strength I have to help Bill Metzger and he can help me, then we'll both make it "

God's assurance so underscored my confidence that we would make it that I rapidly became known as the camp optimist. In fact, this attitude became my mainstay and eventually a contagion which infected others in that dreary camp. In my very limited contacts with other incarcerated Americans, they would ask me, "When do you think we'll be going home, Red?"

"In about two months," I would answer in the upbeat. I lost a lot of credibility as the years dragged on, but they gleaned hope out of my tireless role as the "Positive Rumormonger" anyway. I was kind of a reverse version of the boy who cried wolf.

It was optimism not built on the sand or the platitudes of wishful thinking, but on the bedrock of a solid faith in the assurances of God. It was a rock solid faith that didn't waver with the passing of time but grew steadily stronger and sharper under the relentless pressures of our confinement. Even in a place where tomorrows seemed so dismal, where life and death hung so precariously in the balance, His grace sustained me. Though every effort was exerted to exploit our weaknesses and undermine faith in God and country, He saw me through and checked the dark clouds of despair. Through Him, I learned to survive and even triumph over the sordid realities of boredom, anxiety, and despair. It was a victory we had to grasp in our imprisonment or resign ourselves to the darkness.

The long days turned into months, and the months drifted into years. I shared with others my long-held belief in the power of positive thinking. They in turn would bolster my spirits as the torture sessions came more often and grew more severe.

But worse than the torture was the isolation, the solitary confinement. Our captors knew they could break our spirits if they kept us separated from one another. They knew that a man can endure more pain if he is linked with others in his suffering; isolated, he becomes weak and vulnerable. To break us was their single-minded mission.

They wanted our minds to be empty and bored so we would be receptive to the brainwashing propaganda that they piped into our cells. Besides the wholesale torture, we were allotted ample doses of freelance harassment to wear us down. Exaggerated statistics of American casualties were broadcast over the camp PA. We were informed of American soldiers defecting to Sweden and we were forced to listen to the "Voice of Vietnam." The "Voice" played melancholy recordings of homesick prisoners to their loved ones, and we were fed all the depressing news from America they could dig up: anti-war demonstrations, assassinations, airline disasters, even news of anti-war delegations from the States.

Still, we struggled to beat the system and outwit the guards. I knew we couldn't survive if we didn't communicate with one another. Any risk was acceptable to me if it held the slightest chance of making contact with others. We went to great lengths to keep the lines of communication open, even though it cost us dearly in repeated trips to the "quiz" room for torture. We invented a "tapping code" which we used to stay in touch with other prisoners through the walls and down the corridor, in the washrooms, and under the doors. Besides the camp code, we had other subtle signals such as cough codes, finger signs, clothes swaps, and thumping signals in the dirt with our reed brooms when we swept the courtyard. We even attached scribbled messages on scraps of paper to the underside of our toilet bowls that were placed outside our cells for pick-up. We affectionately called it our "pony express."

With our crude camp code, we tapped out short messages through the thick concrete walls. We shared stories, Bible verses, poems—anything we could think of to help each other cope with the dark hours. We even shared jokes to cheer one another up. Rapid taps signified laughter, while slow, heavy thumps indicated it was a dud. When a man came back from torture, needing encouragement, sometimes needing forgiveness because he hadn't measured up to his own expectations, we tapped our meager moral support to him through those thick walls. It was our way of redeeming a bit of moral victory from the system.

Between the pressure and pain were monotonous gray gaps—tedious hours of boredom, endless hours of nothing to do but think and wonder and sometimes worry. To combat the mind-numbing dullness, we invented elaborate mental exercises to while away the time. We taxed our ingenuity and mental resourcefulness by playing mind games, doing calculations, remembering, planning construction projects, planning vacations, thinking through adventures and fantasies, reliving history, composing poems—anything to keep our minds alert and active.

On Sunday mornings, we worshiped the Lord together, tapping our clandestine worship through the walls. We found bits and pieces of Scripture buried deep inside our minds and shared them with one another—missing words, missing lines, passages paraphrased. We prayed together, through the walls. Then we closed our primitive worship service facing the east, each man in his own cell, toward the Gulf of Tonkin where we knew US Navy ships were waiting offshore, as we pledged our allegiance to our unseen flag.

We learned to pray for our guards, Spot and Rabbit, Jawbone and

Sweetpea, Slug and the others who inflicted such ruthless torture on us. We learned to share our sparse food, to tend another man's wounds, to find and share the courage and strength we needed to meet each day.

We put together, as best we could, a makeshift copy of the Bible. We called it the Revised Prison Version. We wrote down all the Scripture we could recall on pieces of toilet paper stuck together with glutinous rice. Ink was a problem. We tried brick dust and water. We tried blood and water. Finally, we tried cigarette ashes and water, and that worked. The VC gave us three cigarettes a day in the good times when they were feeling generous and we found all kinds of uses for the tobacco. The nicotine was used to clear up toothaches and intestinal parasites. It may not have been effective, but we liked to think it was.

I made a conscious effort not to think about the past and not to dream too much about the future. I knew I had to take one day at a time. I tried to put the good life behind me, to meet each new crisis and each new challenge with all the strength I could muster.

Two things weighed heavily upon my mind. What happened to Kelly the day we bailed out? At every interrogation session, I asked about Kelly. The VC always claimed to have no knowledge of him. We had what we thought was a pretty good system of information in the prison network, but I never was able to ferret out any word about Kelly. And I wondered about Dorothy. Did she know I was still alive? Was there any way I could let her know I was in a POW camp? Since I couldn't think of a way, I was thankful that she at least had the knowledge that I had gotten out of my plane after we had been hit.

Through all of this, I was acutely aware that my struggle for survival was a learning time for me. I would never again be the same man. I would benefit in many ways from my suffering. I would appreciate my country and my freedom when, and if, I ever experienced freedom again. I knew it couldn't go on forever and that in the end our country would free us and not forsake us. I always believed my country would come to get me someday. But I wondered when, and I wondered how.

In 1968, when the bomber missions stopped coming, our hopes soared with a new wave of optimism. The Paris peace talks had begun unbeknownst to us. *We're going home,* I thought. As the weeks and months ticked by and the bombers didn't return, it was hard to hang on to that slender thread of hope. But I knew if I let go, I would not make it through this. And so I did hang on. And I was making it, one day at a time. After every torture session, I would thank God that I was still alive. I would thank Him that I had resisted once again. And I would cling to my belief that my country would never abandon me. I was making it. I would make it. Some day I would go home.

Then came the summer of 1969. I had taken my place as the main communications liaison between two camps. The VC had shuttled us from camp to camp to disrupt our organization and communications system. Early in 1969, they moved me from the Hanoi Hilton to the Zoo Annex, and then over to the compound directly behind the Annex. From my cell, I could see my old cell in the Zoo Annex and was familiar with the layout of both camps. From my new vantage point, I could link the men in both camps to our communications system.

All of this meant that I knew the inner workings of what was secretly going on in both camps. It also meant the Vietnamese knew I knew. Consequently, when John Dramesi and Ed Atterbury got caught in a desperate attempt to escape and were returned to the camp for punishment, the authorities came down hard. They retaliated with an unprecedented vengeance. Some of the men were tortured to death in the enemy's attempt to finger the escape committee.

After they'd beaten their way through about twenty-four men, I was taken to an interrogation room called the "chicken coop" to confirm the information that had been extracted from the others under sadistic torture. Some of what they wanted, I had—some, I didn't. Our captors were in a brutal disposition and determined to get me to say what they wanted me to say. But I was equally determined to resist, even if it cost me my life. As they prodded me to the torture room at the point of a bayonet, I kept telling myself, "I've made it this far. I can still make it." I gritted my teeth and prepared for the worst.

I was placed in loop-shaped U-bolt leg irons intertwining both ankles. My arms were locked behind my back with wrist irons. For the next seven days and nights, I was ruthlessly beaten in that torture room with no sleep and almost no food. I was forced to strip, then sprawl spread-eagle on the floor with my buttocks exposed to repeated blows from a three-and-a-half-foot rubber fan belt until my buttocks became a bloody pulp. I was subjected to relentless demands for information, karate chops, and tire sandal slappings across the face. I was beaten with bamboo sticks and suspended from an overhead beam in agonizing positions with those dreaded ropes until the bone in my left arm snapped. My face, mouth, arms, shoulders, legs, and open wounds were pulsing with pain. My body was wracked with fever, but I refused to give in to their demands. Then they tied cords around my arms and chest, wrapped wet cloths around the cords, and hooked the wires up to a battery. Each time the wires were touched to terminals, violent jabs of voltage jerked my body into spasms. After a week of unrelenting torment, I began to slip in and out of consciousness, occasionally drifting into hallucinations.

At some point during the seventh night, I became aware that I wasn't going to make it after all. All the positive thinking, optimism, and hope I had so carefully nurtured was gone. I was going to die and death would be welcomed.

As I knelt crumpled on the floor in my own blood and wastes, I found myself yielding control to God. I found myself surrendering my fate to Him unconditionally. There was no more human resolve or pride or tenacity of spirit—just surrender to Him. "Lord . . . it's all Yours . . . whatever this means, whatever it is supposed to accomplish in me, whatever You have in mind now with all of this, it's all Yours. . . ." Suddenly the torture stopped at the threshold of death. He had a larger purpose for me. He had spared me at my shootdown. He had graciously allowed me the privilege of serving beside men of great courage—to help them find strength, and to receive strength from them in turn. He had preserved me through two long years of torture and deprivation. He delivered me that seventh night, as well. Kneeling there, empty before God, I was overwhelmed by the sheer power of His presence and profound awareness. He was forging a deeper dimension of faith and commitment in my life to glorify Him in the years ahead.

To my amazement, I was put in a cell with Windy Rivers and Ron Bliss, two outstanding Christians. They didn't recognize me at first because I looked like a specter out of hell. My eyes were sunken, my skin jaundiced, legs pitifully swollen, body caked with scabs and sores, and my hands dangling limply at my sides. But they rallied on my behalf and lovingly nursed me back to health. They fed me, shaved me, washed my wounded body, and more. Jack Van Loan, another prisoner, massaged my hands for hours on end over several months, slowly bringing back circulation. During that time, my broken arm finally began to heal.

The VC left me alone for the next five or six months. And then one day, the dreaded turnkey came and escorted me back to the interrogation room. I was still very weak, and I knew I would not survive another torture session. "Write a letter confessing to your war crimes," Spot demanded, "and we'll let your family know you are still alive." I refused. "You know we can force you," he said.

"You will have to force me," I answered. I knew "force you" meant "torture you," and I knew they were more than qualified to physically destroy me in methodical, maniacal stages.

"But when we force you, it makes us look bad in the eyes of the world," Spot replied. That was a very strange statement coming from him, I thought. And I decided someone, somewhere, was talking about us. Somewhere, in the real world, someone was aware of our plight, and I thought, surely this is the beginning of the end.

It wasn't the end. I would spend three more years in captivity. But there was no more torture. The public outcry back home was putting pressure on Hanoi to improve our treatment. The food was better. I got some mail from home, and I was allowed to write to my family to let them know I was alive. The North Vietnamese were trying to manipulate the world's press and reap the propaganda value of giving the illusion that they were giving the American POWs "humane and lenient" treatment. However, our living conditions only marginally and seasonally improved during the next three years.

On December 18, 1972, the B-52s returned. For the next twelve days, they came around the clock, one wave after another, rocking Hanoi with earth-rending concussions. The massive bombing strikes were a sign our government was fed up with the stalling. They turned up the heat to force the North Vietnamese to negotiate a peace settlement in Paris. Our hopes were rekindled. The punitive air strikes were a clear signal that we would soon be freed.

I began to wonder. After six long years in a Communist prison, where would I fit back home? And what about my family? What kind of toll had this separation taken on them? Would I be a stranger in my own home? What about my shipmates? My squadron? My country? Would there be a place for me? But most of all, would I be able to share, in some small way, what I learned in the darkest hours of a prison cell? For the believer there is no such thing as solitary confinement. As Corrie Ten Boom—a WWII prisoner—once said, "No pit is so deep that God is not deeper still."

In January, we knew we were really going home. Early on the morning of March 4, we were herded into a bus and driven to the Gia Lam airport in Hanoi to board our freedom bird for home. When I saw the waiting C-141 on the field, I choked with emotion as warm tears streaked down my face. The knowledge that our country had not abandoned us was moving, but even more so the awareness of the Lord's words, "I will never leave you nor forsake you," was overwhelming. As I waited in line, I scanned the familiar faces of the guards. I saw Spot, his face unreadable as he watched me move along the line toward my moment of freedom. He had locked me in my cell at night. He had withheld my meager rations, beaten me in the torture room, watched me bleed and almost die. The guards had always seemed so heartless, so stoical. In those six years, we saw no compassion, no tenderness, and no human decency. Out of the same mouth they would tell us, "I am here to give you your rations and bury you when you die." Now he stood along with the others—the guards, the interrogators, the skilled purveyors of torture—and silently watched us go.

For six long years—2,110 days—the little stone-faced men had been my tormentors. What were they thinking as they watched the long-term inmates of the Hanoi Hilton file by? They had performed their tasks well. They had broken the wills and the spirits of a long list of proud men. They had broken the bodies of others. And they had snuffed out the last breath of life in the bravest of us. Were they glad to see us go, to be relieved, finally, of their charges? Were they preparing, even now, to go on to their next assignment, as I was—to do their part in advancing their cause? Were they thinking, as I was, of returning home to their families and to some semblance of normal life outside prison walls?

From the Hanoi Hilton, Zoo, and the other POW camps in North Vietnam, I had tried to fathom the thoughts of these inscrutable men. I had lain on my board-bed on sleepless nights and said to myself, "If I can get a handle on how they think, I'll be able to anticipate, to prepare for the next interrogation." But they were always unpredictable and mercurial in their reactions toward us. Now as I waited for release, I wondered about their lives. I thought of them, for the first time, as men. I was going home to my family and freedom, while they would never know the joy of breathing free. They were prisoners too, victims of a brutal, harsh system that controlled their actions just as they had tried to control mine for so long. As I shuffled across the tarmac, I felt no gloating, only pity.

My turn came. "Welcome home, Commander McDaniel!" The Air Force colonel smiled broadly as he shook my hand. I was free! As the C-141 lifted off, my thoughts turned once more to home and what would await me there. The jet ascended over the familiar green jungle heading for the coast. When we reached the Gulf of Tonkin, all pandemonium broke loose aboard with choruses of "Feet wet!" The roar was deafening. It was a roar of men now free. It came from deep in our souls. Pent-up emotions, years in the building, released the familiar cry, from long-ago days of combat missions, "Feet wet!"

Over the water, out of North Vietnam, we were free!

On the long flight home, I thought of Kelly and others like him who were not among us—still missing—brave men who had died in the jungles, in the torture rooms, in the solitary cells, alone. Or so I believed. "Why me, God? Why not Kelly?"

We landed at Clark Air Force Base in the Philippines for medical tests and intelligence debriefings. My forty-five minutes on the telephone with Dorothy and our children left questions still unanswered. *Where do I fit?* I wondered. But four days into freedom I gathered them into my arms—Dorothy, Mike, David, and Leslie—and I knew that I did fit. I knew that all the strains and uncertainties of my absence had not sullied or soiled our relationship. All the hell of six years couldn't destroy the love between us.

I left with no bitterness. God had allowed the non-crisis cadence of my life to be thrown off. I had been broken in prison and brought to the end of myself under the hands of my captors. Yet it was not man but God who shaped me through the sufferings so that I could minister to others in pain. Someone once said that "before a man can become bread to feed the multitudes, he must first be ground under the millstones of life." I was returning to pick up the pieces of my life a better man—a man with a new depth of sensitivity who could empathize with the suffering of others. I was carrying back knowledge birthed through affliction that "all things" do "work together for good to those who love God."

(Reprinted from Kimball, William, *Vietnam: The Other Side of Glory*, Flemming H. Revell, used by permission.)

A TIME
TO LOVE

*He who does not love does not know
God, for God is love.*
The Apostle John (1 John 4:8)

Love, like virtue, is its own reward.
John Vanbrugh

*Love rules his kingdom without a
sword.*
George Herbert

Love is, above all, the gift of oneself.
Jean Anouilh

The Bread Is in Our Hands

★

And Jesus said to them, "I am the bread of life. He who comes to Me shall never hunger, and he who believes in Me shall never thirst" (John 6:35).

In the 1990s, the revolution in Yugoslavia seemed very remote, until an army nurse related the tales of children who had lived through the siege of Sarejevo. That brought the war home to me.

It surprised me that a story of such magnitude could escape the world's notice.

You see, the children in Sarejevo lived through several years of dehumanizing want: want of heat, food, clothing, peaceful streets. Grief, remorse, death—this was their daily bread. Victims were numerous and random and included both young and old.

When the siege was lifted, many seemingly well children needed hospitalization. The ones who survived those terrible years exhibited overwhelming fear. One of their most prevailing fears was going hungry. Hunger was a powerful and terrible reminder of all they had faced during that violent time. It was the most immediate challenge the army nurses at the hospitals faced in dealing with these little ones.

Complicating their treatment were the memories of nightly gunfire and cries in the dark. The fact they had been removed from the environment they had become accustomed to seemed to increase their fears. *What will happen in this new environment? Will someone hurt us? Will they take away our family or friends?*

Each night, when the lights went out, the wards would echo with the sounds of sobbing children. For many nights the nurses struggled to comfort and console all of these wounded children. What could they do to alleviate their fears? They tried a number of ideas that all seemed to help but not completely solve the cries of sobbing children. One of the nurses finally hit upon the answer. They were afraid of hunger! They never knew whether or not their last meal was truly their *last* meal.

This surprised the nurses because all of the children had been well fed at dinner. The meals came regularly and were more than ample. Yet, the children cried and couldn't be consoled. Feeding children who have been malnourished and near starvation is just the beginning of dealing with hunger. Beyond that, they must begin to trust that more food will be provided when they hunger again. The problem in this case was that children had seen others die during those terrible years. The fear that they too might succumb was an ever-present whisper nagging at their minds.

In a remarkably creative manner, the army nurses discovered a way of quieting their fears and helping them go to sleep. That night, before the lights were put out, the nurses went up and down the wards carefully placing a slice of bread in each child's hand. And then they looked around to ensure no one had been forgotten. The moment had come. They turned out the lights and waited. Soon, the sound of regular rhythmic breathing filled the hospital ward. The children had gone to sleep. They no longer feared the hunger that had been their constant companion. *The bread was in their hands.*

Isn't that where God placed His Son? He wasn't too far off in a distant heaven. He came here to us, within our reach and understanding. He alone can comfort our fears. The bread is in our hands.

TAKING THE HIGH GROUND

A CUP OF WATER

★

TERI L. DUNNEGAN
USAF WIFE

And if anyone gives a cup of cold water to one of these little ones because he is my disciple, I tell you the truth, he will certainly not lose his reward (Matt. 10:42 NIV).

I had a bad case of "Island Fever" at the end of our tour of duty on Guam. Not that I hadn't enjoyed taking our two small children for walks along postcard beaches, eating sandwiches under swaying palms, or inhaling the flowery fragrances of the trade winds. As nice as that was, there were times when I longed for family, old friends, familiar places, and yes, snow.

Yet at the close of our tour I found myself more restless than usual. Instead of happily counting the days until we were stateside again, I felt uneasy, as though I was missing something. I even began thinking about "religious things." I managed to chalk it up to "Island Fever," which covered everything from mild homesickness to down-right depression.

Moving day finally arrived, along with cardboard boxes, stacks of packing paper, and more people than I could count to pack up our meager belongings. Among the people who showed up was a young officer from the TMO (Transportation Management Office). He explained that he would be supervising our particular packers.

There are only two kinds of days on Guam: very hot and humid and only slightly less than very hot and humid. Moving day fell into the category of very hot and humid. I kept iced tea and Kool-Aid on hand. Everyone availed themselves of the cold drinks—everyone, that is except the TMO officer.

He seemed organized, knowledgeable, and tireless. I began to trust his judgment and I also began to worry about him. In fact, I began to feel almost motherly toward him. He had stood outside in the heat with nothing to drink for a long time. Surely he was thirsty. I asked him twice if I could get him some iced tea or a glass of Kool-Aid. He politely turned me down.

I went outside a third time and pleaded with him to let me bring him a cool drink. He started to say something and then he stopped. He cocked his head to the side, just a little, as if he were listening to something or someone. I was about to repeat my offer when he smiled at me and said, "Yes, I will have a drink." Then he gave specific instructions, "I just want a cup of water. Use whatever cup is handy and fill it with tap water."

I protested. Didn't he want iced tea? No, he didn't. Couldn't I at least put ice in the cup for him? No, I couldn't. I thought it was a rather strange request, but I found a cup and gave him water from the tap. He drank it down, handed me the cup, and smiled beautifully. I didn't have time to mull over his strange request. We were all busy until lunch break.

The TMO officer found a place to sit down and he opened up his briefcase. He took out a brown paper bag, a notebook, and a book.

I ate on the run and passed by him several times. Finally, my curiosity got the better of me and I asked him if he were studying for some kind of class. He chuckled a bit, then said, "Well, I am a student of sorts. You see, I am studying the Bible."

That answer so startled me that I came up with the brilliant reply of "Really!" It had never occurred to me that people, other than preachers, actually studied the Bible.

I didn't know much about the contents of the Bible. I did know that Revelation was the last book in the Bible. I knew that because for some inexplicable reason, just weeks before, I had retrieved a Bible from a box in the hall closet and read the last book. Did I understand what I read? Not really. So maybe what this man was doing was admirable.

Before lunch was over that day, two friends arrived. In almost reverent tones I told them that he was actually studying the Bible. They laughed and I got angry. I told them that he was probably better than the three of us put together. For the rest of the day they treated me as one would a crazy relative on leave from a mental institution.

Throughout the next few weeks, I kept thinking about the TMO officer reading his Bible and asking for a simple cup of water. I wondered why. We settled in at our new base and I met a teacher—a teacher who read her Bible also. This woman showed me what Christ really does for a person, and I became a Christian and began to study the Bible.

I found it exciting and wondrous. I also found the verse about those that give a cup of water to God's children (Matt. 10:42). It was at that point that I understood. The young TMO officer had been listening to God. He remembered that verse, and I received a blessing. God had used him to help convict me of my need for the Savior.

That was twenty years ago, and I am still amazed at what God can do with an obedient Christian and a cup of water.

(Used by permission of Command magazine, published by Officers' Christian Fellowship, Englewood, Colorado.)

A LESSON IN FRIENDSHIP

★

A man who has friends must himself be friendly,
But there is a friend who sticks closer than a brother (Prov. 18:24).

There is a great lesson in how the treasury department trains its employees to distinguish real currency from counterfeit. The agents spend days carefully examining piles of genuine bills. After a thorough familiarity is achieved, supervisors begin to introduce counterfeits into piles. Without too much difficulty, the agents are able to spot the counterfeit because they have become so familiar with the "real thing."

When it came to friendship, I don't believe I had ever seen the real thing. I'd caught glimpses of it from time to time, but not in any way that captured my attention. That was to change when I met a man named Lee.

The air force had transferred me from the state I'd grown up in to the untamed land of Alaska. Everything about it was different. In the winter, you plugged your car into an outlet to keep the oil from freezing. In the summer, you pulled down blinds at night because the sun never set. The forbidding and often unforgiving land around you was equally matched with a hospitality I'd not seen before.

We bought a house in North Pole, Alaska, and faced the formidable event called "moving-in day"—again. This was our seventh move in nine years of marriage, and we'd grown somewhat used to the rigors of being regularly displaced. Military families usually can count on others when moving into on-base quarters. There's always someone around to lend you a hand if you need it. But we were moving into a house thirteen miles away from the base and knew absolutely no one.

The night before we moved in, we made one more trip to the house. We were going to bring a few items over and make sure all was ready for the moving truck. As we arrived, our neighbors came over to greet us. Lee led them. He had sold his house to us and moved into a new house two doors down the week before.

He said, rather matter of factly, "We're here to help." I told him that was nice, "But the movers won't be here until the morning," I advised him.

"No you don't understand," he replied. "We're here to clean your house from top to bottom, and then we're going to paint the inside for you. Is white okay?"

My wife and I were astonished. Three sets of neighbors set to work cleaning the house. About midnight the cleaning was done and the paintbrushes came out. Four hours later the entire interior of the house had a fresh coat of paint. Three hours later the movers arrived. This outpouring of Christian love overwhelmed us.

Getting used to the new environment in Alaska took some time. During the winter, garages are heated to keep the oil in the cars from freezing. Further, since many homes—including ours—had wells, the well pump was also in the heated garage to keep it from freezing.

My wife arrived home one evening from a long day of teaching school. Somehow as she came into the house, she forgot to close the garage door. At 5:00 the next morning, I went into the shower, turned on the faucet and got—nothing. A little dribble of water came out. I went downstairs and out into the garage. My eyes must have bugged out when I saw the garage door standing wide open.

I closed it and then looked into the pump room. Solid ice covered the pump. I was floored. My wife was beside herself. I looked at the clock as I dialed my friend Lee. It was 5:30 am. I thought, he'll know what to do. I related our situation and he said, "Don't worry about it. I'll get some tools and be over in a few minutes." Within a half hour, Lee had arrived and started cleanup operations. He helped us heat the garage and drain the pump. Water spewed all over the floor creating more ice as he dismantled the pump. Lee pulled out the cracked and broken parts and went to town to purchase replacements. By noon that day, he had the pump back up and running and, for the price of parts, I had learned two important lessons.

First, and obviously, close the garage door in winter! But more importantly, I learned the meaning of real friendship. Lee has been my example of a friend as I've gone from assignment to assignment. In my own way, I've tried to be a friend to others. I'm warmed by the memory of his friendship. I feel warmer still, knowing he remains a friend today, fifteen years later.

LOVE COVERS ALL

★

TERI DUNNEGAN
USAF WIFE

And walk in love, as Christ also has loved us and given Himself for us, an offering and a sacrifice to God for a sweet-smelling aroma (Eph. 5:2).

I am always amazed at how God's most significant lessons take place in the most common settings. From the moment He came to earth, His message was contained in a manger in an animal barn. I think it pleases the Lord that we need to seek Him to discover His truths.

During my morning devotions, I pondered this verse: "Above all love each other deeply, because love covers a multitude of sins" (1 Peter 4:8 NIV). I kept on reading, but that one sentence perplexed me. I finally gave up reading any more scripture and dug a little deeper.

How does that work? I wondered. *We aren't supposed to cover up sins, are we? How could loving someone, however deeply, cover sin?* The only cover for sin I knew of was Jesus. Which brought me back to, *How does that work?*

I prayed for wisdom, and although I didn't get an immediate flash of insight, I figured the Lord would make things clear sooner or later.

I went to pick up my daughter at the base childcare center that afternoon. Since I worked in the opposite direction, this was usually my husband's job. However, he was flying that day so I made the lengthy cross-town trip.

When I walked into the reception area there were two men ahead of me. The man at the head of the line was obviously unhappy and was loud and rude to the woman behind the counter. After throwing several verbal rocks at the poor woman, he gathered up his children along with their belongings and left.

I felt sorry for the woman behind the counter until she expressed her anger and humiliation by flinging harsh words at the man who was next in line. Then I began to feel sorry for myself and my daughter. After all, I was next. Her angry face told me that I wasn't going to get any better treatment than the fellow ahead of me.

It was my turn. I had only seconds before I would be faced with an angry caregiver. So I prayed. You know the kind of prayer I am talking about. That frantic, desperate "I need help *now*, Lord," kind of prayer we all have to pray from time to time.

Help came and things changed. However, what changed wasn't the visible circumstances around me. What changed was my perception of them. In a moment, I no longer saw an angry young woman. Instead, I saw a very tired woman. She was worn out from the events of the day. She was tired of running in place. I saw a woman the Lord loved and wanted to gather into His comforting arms.

I still wasn't quite sure what to do, but before she could say anything, I managed to speak. Taking a deep breath, I stepped up to the counter and quietly said, "My, you sure have had a tough day today, haven't you?"

Not exactly earth shaking or particularly eloquent words of wisdom, but they seemed to have an impact. I watched as her angry face crumbled. Her whole body seemed to shrink. She leaned on the counter and rested her chin on her hand, and wearily said, "You have no idea."

There was no one behind me in line, so for the next minute or two, she vented and I sympathized. Finally, I patted her on the hand, said, "Bless your heart, you really have had a bad time. Life sure can get hectic in a hurry. If you like, I'll say a prayer for you."

At first she seemed a little startled, then she seemed to like the idea and said, "Thanks, I certainly need all the prayers I can get." She turned around and went to get my daughter.

While I was waiting, I began to pray for her. No sooner had I finished praying than God reminded me of the verse I studied that morning. The same verse that perplexed me earlier now became clear as the morning sky. I could feel myself smiling. God had answered my prayer for wisdom by giving me an object lesson.

When the woman came back with my daughter, I mentioned

that I had prayed for her. She thanked me again. I took my daughter's hand, and said good-bye. As I turned to walk away, another parent came in. Before I walked out the door, I overheard her begin to speak. Her tone and demeanor had completely changed. She was no longer a worn out, angry woman. Instead, God had refreshed her through the minutes we had spent together. She was able to pass that refreshment on to the next parent who came through the door that night.

I smiled at my daughter as we held hands and headed out the door. God had revealed the truth of His word to me. Love had covered the hurt and sin in the most ordinary of circumstances that day.

A TIME
TO BUILD UP

In a just cause the weak will beat the strong.
Sophocles

A chain is no stronger than its weakest link.
English Saying

What does not kill me makes me stronger.
Friedrich Nietzsche

ANGELS AMONG US

★

LT. COL. BILL BIERBAUM
USAF

For he shall give his angels charge over you,
to keep you in all your ways (Ps. 91:11).

My dream had finally come true. After a grueling year of training, I graduated from flight school and received my wings. My wife and I, along with a friend, left the mild winter weather of California as we headed for the frozen plains of central Alaska.

We boarded a ferry and stood on the stern as we watched Seattle disappear into the fog. This sea journey was in itself quite an adventure for two small-town midwesterners. It was also a humbling experience watching civilization disappear in the distance. My wife, Gina, and I held each other and I reassured her everything would be fine, all the time wondering about our future. I asked the Lord, as I have throughout my life, to take care of us. All in all, the three-day trip along the Alaskan marine highway was both beautiful and relaxing.

Our ferry deposited us along with our vehicles at Haines, Alaska. We left that morning confident we'd enjoy a scenic day of travel. In a few hours we entered the Canadian Rockies, every bit as formidable as the Rocky Mountains of Colorado. Gina flipped the radio dial and heard that the Canadian authorities were closing a mountain pass due to an impending snow storm. My heart jumped as I realized this was the very road we were on!

The next few minutes seemed to assure us that the weatherman was wrong again. Nothing seemed out of the ordinary as I carefully scanned the horizon ahead. Then without warning, a blowing snowstorm engulfed us. The road rapidly disappeared beneath icy snow and visibility shrank until I could no longer see even a few feet in front of the windshield.

I had no choice but to stop. We were high on the mountain with the cliff's edge next to the car door. I went back to see my friend and ask his opinion. We decided to stay put, and I found my way back to my car by running my hand along the edge until I reached the driver's door.

I settled into my seat and looked at Gina. I asked the Lord to take care of us and give us the strength to make it out of the storm safely. We sat in the car for what seemed a very long time. There was little more I could do now. I began to wonder about running out of gas. What would it be like to be frozen and not found until the spring thaw? What if we had a flat tire? *What if? What if? What if?* I considered a myriad of catastrophes that might occur.

Faintly and then more loudly, I heard an approaching vehicle. I hoped it had room to pass without hitting us. I couldn't see well enough to know what would happen. And then, it was upon us—a huge truck with a snowplow passed us and then stopped. The driver came up to my window and told me to follow his truck and to keep my eyes on the yellow light. I did as instructed, thankful to our rescuer. My friend followed me using my taillights to guide him. I followed the yellow light as it weaved back and forth along the road.

Without warning, we broke through the snow and fog as suddenly as it had come upon us. The road ahead of us was clear. No fog, no ice, no stalled vehicles. We stopped our cars, got out, and hugged each other.

But where was the yellow snowplow and the driver who had led us to safety? The snowplow, driver, and yellow light were gone. They had vanished. We looked around and couldn't figure out a road where he could have turned off to have disappeared so quickly.

As I thought about it later I reasoned his disappearance was impossible. I *never* lost sight of the snowplow until we were out of the storm. The driver and truck were gone.

As we continued our journey north, we discussed the storm and our amazing deliverance. The rest of our trip was cold, beautiful, and thankfully, uneventful.

On cold winter days, I still ponder our trip to Alaska. Did God send an angel to rescue us high up on that snow covered mountain pass? The Book of Hebrews tells us "Are they not all ministering spirits sent forth to minister for those who will inherit salvation?" I'm one who believes the answer to that question is an unqualified "Yes!"

Mom to Mom

★

SARAH HEMINGWAY
USMC WIFE

Two are better than one, because they have a good return
for their labor. For if either of them falls, the one will lift up
his companion. But woe to the one who falls when there is not
another to lift him up (Ecc. 4: 9-10 NASB).

It's hard to remember the exact moment Jenny McDonald came into my life. I think we met at a church picnic on the beach. My husband, Tom, had just returned from his second tour of duty in Vietnam. Jenny's husband, Mike, a former marine, had just been accepted at the Los Angeles Police Academy. We had little girls, four and two years old, and they had a three-year-old daughter and a newborn son. It was one of those preordained meetings when God delightfully slips someone special into our lives.

Our friendship blossomed as much out of our need for each other as anything else. We were young couples trying to follow God, raise children, and stay within our limited budgets. We began to talk frankly with each other about our victories and frustrations in raising our families. Some days were wonderful—potty training was a success. Some days were dreadful—chicken pox and sleepless nights took their toll. What a gift it was to know another family understood what we were going through.

Soon the McDonalds moved closer to our area, and Mike began his first police assignment. My friendship with Jenny grew. When I had a doctor's appointment, she insisted I bring our girls to her house. When she needed to shop, she dropped Susie and Scott off at my house.

While I tidied up my house for other people, I felt totally comfortable when Jenny came in and stepped over the toys and clutter. I knew she understood because her house was "decorated" the same way. I remember the day I woke up miserably sick with the flu. One phone call to her, and she was gathering up my children, telling them what a wonderful day they were going to have, and asking them what their favorite cereal was. She returned that evening with dinner prepared for us.

We compared information of every kind. I introduced her to a children's park I discovered. She told me about the Japanese lady who grew a field of flowers and sold lovely bouquets for a dollar. We compared notes on strep throat symptoms. Between tending skinned knees and making peanut butter and jelly sandwiches, we discussed what it meant to raise children to love God. We exchanged victories and failures, as well as recipes, spiritual truths, discipline techniques, and encouraging Bible verses.

Three weeks before our third baby was due, Tom and I were in the middle of house redecorating projects when I went into labor. With a couch still in the middle of the hall, we left for the hospital and had our third child. Jenny visited in the hospital, beaming as she shared our joy. Little did I know that I would come home to an immaculate house, compliments of my sneaky friend!

On another occasion, I had fallen woefully behind in preparing for the arrival of my in-laws who were due the next day. At nine that morning the doorbell rang. Standing at the door was my pal in hilarious cleaning garb, complete with a red bandanna tied around her head. "Did you send for a maid?" She grinned.

At that time, my relatives lived thousands of miles away. Hers did too. I know I was as much of a help to Jenny as she was to me. When Mike was on duty and she was afraid, she called—even at midnight—and we prayed for her and for his safety on the job.

Jenny McDonald wasn't college educated. She wasn't president of a club or a member of a professional organization. She wasn't a super-mom either. That was the beauty of it. It's just that God was able to use us in each other's lives in the most ordinary ways: to help, encourage, console, and cheer.

Sometimes the face of Jesus is found in a friend. If you were to ask where the love of Jesus was at that time in my life, I would answer, "He's showing His love to me through Jenny." Many of us in the military are far from relatives. Sometimes we get tired and discouraged. Many of us are on budgets and often can't afford a babysitter. But we have each other. Where one is weak, another is strong.

(Used by permission of Command magazine, published by Officers' Christian Fellowship, Englewood, Colorado.)

FROM CORPS TO CORE — OUR VALUES, OUR FAITH

★

DR. DENNIS HENSLEY
US ARMY 1970-1971

Thy word have I hid in mine heart,
that I might not sin against thee (Ps. 119:11 KJV).

For three long, arduous months our twenty-two-year-old, college-graduate son withstood the rigors of Marine Corps boot camp. On graduation day my wife and I were in the grandstands in San Diego to observe the ceremony. At its conclusion, everyone rushed onto the parade ground to find loved ones and offer congratulations.

We found our son. He was tan, muscular, and square-jawed. His uniform was creased to perfection, his shoes were glossy, and his hat was snow white and pulled forward. He looked, stood, and talked like the marine he was. We could read the pride of accomplishment in his face. His class had begun with a full contingency of strong and motivated young men, yet twenty-one percent had not made it through boot camp. Our Nathan was now one of "the few, the proud."

As we spent the rest of the day touring the base, we could tell that our son had been engrained with the values of the Marine Corps—honor, bravery, duty, honesty, commitment, respect, discipline. Nowhere was this more evident than when we took time to tour the Marine Corps Museum. As we strolled from one exhibit to the next, our son would point to a wall poster or a full-size mural and say, "And this was when we charged up Iwo Jima in March of 1945" and "This was when we held off the Viet Cong attack against the US embassy in Saigon in 1968."

My wife and I looked curiously at each other. We? Was he actually saying "we" had done all these heroic deeds? Our son was only twenty-two, yet in just three months a sense of Marine Corps identity had been instilled so deeply in him, he was speaking as though he had had a part in making the Corps what it was. His drill instructors had impressed upon him both the dignity and the responsibility that came with donning the uniform of a United States Marine. He had learned he must never, *ever* do anything that would tarnish the heritage it stood for. "Once a marine, always a marine" was more than just a slogan to these men; it was a lifetime commitment.

On our flight back to Indiana, I couldn't help drawing a comparison between marines and people of the Christian faith. The marines, noble though they are, have only two hundred years of history, whereas Christians have two *thousand* years of history behind them. Shouldn't Christians, then, be even more readily identifiable than marines?

Shouldn't our Christian traits of love, charity, humility, and righteousness be as obvious in our character as the traits of bravery and honor are in a marine?

If in three months of indoctrination the Marine Corps can completely change the heart and mind of a recruit, shouldn't a lifetime of Bible study and prayer change the hearts and minds of followers of Christ?

They say a marine can be spotted even out of uniform—the short haircut, the straight posture, the rugged physique are all traits that immediately identify them. So, what about us? Would we be "spotted" as Christians in the workplace, the neighborhood, the shopping mall, the schools? Do we need to be carrying a Bible or sitting in a pew to make ourselves obvious?

No, not if we, too, undergo daily training. David said, "Thy word have I hid in mine heart, that I might not sin against thee" (Ps. 119:11 KJV). Our Christian "core" values, *our visible life*, the level of our devotion to that training, will be our evidence.

HONOR YOUR
FATHER AND MOTHER

★

*Honor your father and your mother, as the Lord your God has
commanded you, that your days may be long, and that it may
be well with you in the land which the Lord your God is
giving you* (Deut. 5:16).

As children grow older, they've been known to discover their parents get wiser and wiser. While parents learn a lot along the way, the steepest learning curve (as all parents will tell you) occurs in the child. I was no exception, though living with my dad was no picnic. To many children, it seems strange that the scriptural admonition to honor our mothers and fathers doesn't make exceptions for parents who are less than perfect. So, as a child grows older, the question is, "how do you honor a parent whose personality and behavior have so annoyed you growing up?" For some, the annoyance goes on well into adulthood, yet the scriptural admonition still remains.

My father served the navy for more than twenty-one years through two major wars. He joined the navy at seventeen, just as the US entered WWII. He sought something more exciting than following in his father's footsteps delivering dairy products in western Massachusetts. As a child, I came to know him as a hard man—short-tempered, easily angered, and definitely unpredictable. In truth, I lived in great fear of him until after I became a Christian at age sixteen. As the years passed, I also came to know him as a very compassionate man with a very generous heart.

My father retired from the navy feeling angry and disappointed with his treatment. He had pulled many sea tours, and, as one achieved seniority, the time at sea usually diminished. For him this didn't occur. In fact, once he put in his retirement papers, he was sent back to sea with increasing frequency. It wasn't uncommon for him to arrive back in the afternoon from one tour and be put on another ship the next day to go back to sea. This was the environment he faced as his retirement day approached.

After twenty-one years of service, he told his commanding officer he didn't want a retirement ceremony. His words were more harsh than I could write here, but most who serve in the military can imagine what they were. Even his final day was quite contentious as he was run from place to place for signatures that were provided only grudgingly and with delay.

Consequently, he left with a bad opinion of the navy and his military experience. My dad had served not just honorably, but with valor, being decorated with the bronze star for action under fire.

It took me many years to see my dad beneath the tough exterior he exuded. After entering the service myself, I slowly saw military life as it was—both its possibilities and shortcomings. A little more than thirty years after my dad retired, I was selected for promotion to lieutenant colonel. At the time, I was the commander of a 200-person squadron at Officer Training School. Because my mom and dad hadn't been able to attend previous promotion ceremonies, I was excited when they told me they would be flying in for this event. I also saw the possibility of honoring Dad in a special way and helping him find closure to a distinguished career. Perhaps we might write a different ending to what he thought was his final military chapter.

Prior to the promotion ceremony, my parents saw me officiate at the graduation of a class of new second lieutenants. This involved a number of events with pomp and circumstance: parades, a formal dinner, and a B-1 bomber fly-by. Following the final event, my promotion ceremony was held in the hall of heroes where photographs of Medal of Honor winners were displayed. My father and mother sat in the front row, oblivious to what was coming next. Following a review of my career, I was invited forward along with my family to be "pinned" as a lieutenant colonel. I thanked everyone who attended and expressed my appreciation for those who had been influential in my career. And then, the moment arrived.

"I have someone special here who has been influential in ways even he may not realize. This person is my father who retired from the navy some thirty-three years ago. Will Petty Officer First Class

O'Leary please come forward?" At this point, I produced a triangular case with the American flag inside. "I am very proud of what my father accomplished in his career, but am also grateful for the clear footprints he left behind on a path of both distinguished and honorable service. My father, for many reasons, never had a retirement ceremony. In the presence of many soon-to-be officers and newly commissioned officers here today, I believe it in order to present him with a flag of appreciation, from a grateful nation, for his long and distinguished service. Further, I will ask all present to stand to attention as we present him the Bronze Star and read the orders signed by the Commander of the Seventh Fleet and approved by the President of United States."

The Bronze Star Medal is hereby awarded to Henry C. O'Leary for meritorious achievement while serving on the U.S.S. HANNA during combat operations against enemy North Korean and Chinese Communist Forces in the Korean Theater on 24 November 1952. While patrolling a section of the enemy held coast of North Korea, the HANNA was taken under heavy fire by enemy shore batteries. During the ensuing engagement, a fire broke out on the fan tail of the ship, occasioned by the ignition of chemical smoke. The flames greatly endangered the ship because of their close proximity to ordnance material. Due to damage already inflicted on the ship, no water to fight the fire was available in the vicinity. O'Leary, disregarding his personal safety, single-handedly extinguished the fire by beating it out with a piece of canvas, despite the pain and shock occasioned by the ship's after five-inch gun firing in rapid fire directly over his head. The concussion from this gun was such that it completely wrecked a ready service ammunition box in the vicinity. At the same time, enemy shells were exploding in the water repeatedly, at short distance from his exposed position. His outstanding courage, daring initiative, and steadfast devotion to duty were at all times in keeping with the highest traditions of the United States Naval Service.

As the applause rang out, I turned and saluted my dad. I saw a sense of final closure in his eyes for the gratefulness and appreciation he had waited more than thirty years to receive. Many people queued up to congratulate me on my promotion. However, that paled in comparison to the lines of young officers and trainees who shook Dad's hand with a little bit of awe and a profound sense of gratefulness.

A TIME
TO DIE

Any man's death diminishes me
because I am involved in Mankind;
And therefore never send to know for
whom the bell tolls; it tolls for thee.

John Donne

Death plucks my ears and says,
"Live—I am coming."

Virgil

A BREATH IN TIME

★

LT. COL. LYNDON WILLMS
USAF

Peace I leave with you, My peace I give to you;
not as the world gives do I give to you. Let not your heart
be troubled, neither let it be afraid (John 14:27).

President's Day, 1986 was a very dramatic day in my life and brought me closer to the Lord than I ever thought possible.

I was on another deployment to the garden spot of the Pacific and Arctic Oceans—Shemya Island. From there I flew many missions on board the RC 135 (reconnaissance jet). Shemya served as a small allied outpost in the Aleutian Island chain from WWII all the way through the Cold War. Being deployed on President's Day meant I had the day off and time to knock out some reading for my master's degree. Reading back home was difficult since I had become the proud dad of triplets eight months earlier.

Because our triplets had come prematurely, they suffered a lot of complications. Madagan Army Medical Center's Neonatal Intensive Care Unit had been a second home to us during the past months and the staff knew us well.

About ten in the morning, the phone rang and I expected a voice telling me to get my crew ready to fly. The voice at the end of the phone sounded distant and I realized it was a call from the mainland. A doctor introduced himself as an emergency room physician and said, "I'm afraid I have some bad news." All I could think was something had happened to our most ill child, Lindsay. "I'm sorry to tell you that your son, Caleb, has died."

I was numb. I felt distant and detached as I tried to comprehend what I had just heard. The doctor told me some details of Caleb's Sudden Infant Death Syndrome episode but I really didn't understand. My wife came on for just a minute to tell me she loved me and she was okay. I hung up the phone and wished with every aching fiber of my body that I was there with my wife.

What I didn't know was my bigger family, my air force family, was already working to get me home. The on-call alert tanker crew back at Eielson AFB was re-called for duty. An instructor pilot volunteered to bring a KC-135 tanker plane and crew into Shemya, during very hazardous weather conditions. A crew member had volunteered to come out and replace me. By late that afternoon, I was on the plane home as the only passenger.

I had the whole back of the airplane to myself on the three-hour flight home. I crawled into one of the crew rest bunks and started a pity party. I thought about the many struggles Caleb went through and how quickly he was gone. Why couldn't God have kept him and healed him? Why did our family have to go through more pain? Losing a child felt as if someone had ripped a hole in my heart, and the hole felt irreparable.

Then God quietly spoke to my heart using Scripture to calm my fear and grief. "Peace I leave with you, my peace I give unto you: not as the world giveth, give I unto you. Let not your heart be troubled, neither let it be afraid." I felt His presence begin to fill my heart with that peace. I realized I was wrong. That hole could be repaired, and my healing was already beginning.

On arriving home, my wife told me Caleb had been awake and normal just minutes before he stopped breathing. She called the paramedics and started to give him CPR. By God's grace he revived and began to breathe. Amazingly, a paramedic neighbor heard the call over his radio and rushed to our house within two minutes. By the time my wife and the paramedics arrived at the hospital, the first members of our church arrived as well. It was such a blessing to be surrounded by loving friends.

In spite of all the heroic efforts, a few minutes after they got to the ER, the doctor informed my wife he was dead. The medical technician who had tried to save him had tears in his eyes as he carried Caleb's body to the morgue.

It wasn't until years later that I could see God's hand in Caleb's short life. He had been with us for just a moment, a breath, and then he was gone. Caleb touched many lives in the hospital and church as he fought for life. His death broke his grandfather's heart and led him to the Lord. I was able to comfort the father of a cystic fibrosis patient with Caleb's story. Through the short "breath" called Caleb, this father also gave his heart to the Lord.

Someday I'll see my son again. This is more than hope; it is a sure and certain knowledge given to all believers.

WINTER'S RHYTHM

★

LT. COL. BOB MACY (RETIRED)
USAF

To every thing there is a season, and a time to every purpose under the heaven: A time to be born, and a time to die; a time to plant, and a time to pluck up that which is planted (Ecc. 3:1-2 KJV).

It turned out to be the coldest winter any of us could remember, even for Alaska. But the Aleutian Islands were even worse because the winds blew with unabated fury across the bare island. This winter proved colder still as news of trouble reached our distant remoteness.

"Every crew member report to Hangar 2," the loudspeaker boomed. With those words echoing down the halls of our hangar, thirty flyers headed to the briefing room. We flew reconnaissance missions from the small island called Shemya and were part of America's far flung deployed forces. Cold warriors in a cold winter, fighting the Cold War; it all seemed to fit.

I slumped into my seat wondering what the meeting was about. A young captain among others of similar age and rank, I wasn't prepared for the words that followed. The detachment commander walked into the room without his characteristic crispness, gripping the papers he held in his hand. He looked at us sitting there and said quietly, "We've lost an aircraft with three people on board. We lost contact with it in the mountains near Valdez, Alaska. We'll keep you informed as more details become available." I sat there in shock as the obvious question came to everyone's mind. Who was on the aircraft?

The commander soon learned that our squadron operations officer, our senior evaluator pilot and a staff navigator were on the plane. No wreckage had been sighted. However, in the middle of an Alaskan winter high in the mountains, there wasn't much hope. The previous week a blizzard had covered nearly every visible peak with one hundred inches of snow.

I stumbled around the hangar in a fog as I tried to comprehend the fact that three of my squadron mates were not coming home. My mind flashed back to the previous week when I had lounged by a pool at Hickam AFB in Hawaii. Next to me was the evaluator pilot who had just gone missing. We had been pretty close, at least close enough to share our hopes and dreams and even our Christian faith. We soaked up the sun and traded dreams and ideas for almost two hours. He was a strong father, husband, and a real gentleman. I admired him for his walk with God as well as his conduct as an officer. He was a real professional.

Though we attended the same church, Hawaii had been the first real chance to talk about our faith. So many questions flooded my mind. Why did this happen to these men? What would happen to their families? What could I do to help? Were the other two flyers Christians?

As weeks rolled into months, no wreckage was found. The conditions were too severe to conduct a thorough search of the area. I tried to help the family of the pilot I'd come to know. I'd head over to his house when the snow got bad and shovel it off his roof. His wife and three little girls weren't in any condition to perform this important safety procedure. As I threw snow off the roof, I looked down at one of his three daughters and wept. What would happen to her and her sisters?

It wasn't until early August that the snow had melted enough to find the airplane. It was in pieces along the mountainside above Valdez. The three bodies of our fellow flyers were found in the cockpit. Another meeting was called and we were informed that the deaths of our friends had been confirmed. We closed a chapter in our lives that summer when we filed in for the memorial service.

The pastor commended my friend for the acts of service he'd performed and for his complete dedication to Christ. He asked us how we were doing in that department. Had we been giving our lives to His service? I couldn't give a good answer that day. He explained that words and faith without works is just dead faith. That struck me like a bolt. I talked the talk but didn't walk the walk. At twenty-nine, this was a lesson I needed to hear. As I left the church, I felt a new spirit rise up in me. Ever since that day, I have endeavored to serve in such a manner as to leave no doubt as to my faith.

I don't know why God chose to take these men from the earth. Three sets of children grew up without fathers. The thing I came to learn was that winter has its own kind of rhythm. It is both a deadly avalanche and a crisp, quiet snow. I had discovered both life and death that winter. Though my friend was gone, God had awakened my spirit and renewed my heart. I would not be the same.

A COMMANDER'S DARKEST DAY

★

So teach us to number our days,
That we may gain a heart of wisdom (Ps. 90:12).

When you accept the responsibility of being a commander, you really never know what you'll face from the day you assume command until the day you relinquish it. My first experience as a commander was as a young major at the Air Force Academy in Colorado Springs. I was given 125 highly motivated cadets in need of constant direction—all speed and no vector as we used to say. Among the cadets I had were several soccer players. Keeping them moving in the right direction was a pretty tall order.

Kelly[9], was a happy-go-lucky soccer-playing cadet with energy to boot. She lived life and played the game as though they were the same.

The call came at 4:30 a.m. on a cold winter morning. It was from the command post, which relayed a message from a police station north of Colorado Springs. My happy-go-lucky cadet was dead. The questions came quickly. Did I know Kelly? Was I her commander? Did I know she had been out beyond curfew that night? Did I know why she was so far north of the Academy?

I arrived at my office a half hour after the first call and began to gather the facts and make the necessary notifications. For the next six hours my phone must have rung a hundred times. I never answered so many questions with so few facts for so many hours as I did early that Saturday morning. It's hard to imagine, but before the family could be officially notified, they called my office and asked me directly, "Is it true that Kelly is dead?" The air force has a very rigorous procedure for notifying family of a death. The news had spread like wild fire and the rumors had beaten the AF to the family's doorstep. In all my life I couldn't have imagined having to answer such a question. My heart pounded as I passed the terrible truth across the thousand miles that separated us.

Though the facts and details were kept quiet, the rumors swept through the halls of the Academy. A place that was normally bustling and energized took on the appearance of a slow motion, silent movie.

I suppose it didn't surprise me to hear she was off campus on a prank. She had a blood alcohol level well above the legal limit and wasn't wearing her seat belt when her car rolled over and she was crushed.

What I remember most of the days that followed was the reaction of the mother the first time she saw her daughter. We had accompanied her to the funeral home where the body had been prepared and laid out in a casket. The funeral director had done the best he could, but it wasn't possible to remove all traces of the crash. The mother, accompanied by her husband, walked up the aisle looking to the left and to the right until she passed the last pew. Finally, when she was close enough to avoid it no longer, she looked upon her still daughter. A piercing scream filled the chapel and she collapsed. Then she began to wail. It is hard to fully appreciate the depth of such grief until you witness it first hand. My wife and I could only offer our silent presence and heartfelt sympathies. That could hardly fill the gaping hole left by a vibrant daughter now silent in death.

At the memorial service, the chapel filled with grieving cadets and the friends and family of Kelly. Many wondered, *Was there something I could have done to have prevented this?* Silence would be their only comfort. All of us must ultimately take responsibility for our lives. Sadly, Kelly paid the highest price possible for a night of celebration.

We each left the grave site with our own thoughts and grief. The Lord reminded me that it is He who holds our lives and knows the number of our days. I felt spurred on to do what good I could in the days the Lord had given to me. As I drove from the cemetery I silently prayed along with David, "Lord, teach us to number our days."

A TIME
TO HEAL

*An ounce of prevention is worth
a pound of cure.*

Benjamin Franklin

*Nothing refreshes and aids a sick man so
much as the affection of his friends.*

Seneca the Younger

THE FELLOWSHIP OF SUFFERING

★

MAJOR MARK LEE WALTERS
US ARMY

. . .that I may know Him and the power of His resurrection, and the fellowship of His sufferings, being conformed to His death. . .
(Phil. 3:10).

March 23, 1994 started off as an exceptionally great day. If you had asked me what my life's priorities were, I would have told you they were God, Stephanie, and the army. But if you had looked into my schedule book, even a casual observer would have seen otherwise. In fact, both Stephanie and God were competing for my leftovers—leftover time and leftover energy.

That particular morning I didn't spend time with the Lord because there was just too much to do. In two weeks I was going to take command of an airborne rifle company. I felt I needed every available moment to tie up loose ends at work and log as many parachute jumps as I could. I had allowed myself to let the "tyranny of the urgent" take the place of both God and family.

By that afternoon, I was one of about 200 airborne soldiers at Pope AFB conducting pre-flight preparations and rehearsals on the Green Ramp. On that taxi ramp we used aircraft mock-ups to practice the actions we performed in flight. It was a beautiful day, no clouds, the temperature near sixty degrees and the winds low; all in all, a perfect day for a jump.

Without warning our perfect day changed. Above us a C130 Hercules Transport aircraft received approval to land. At the same time, an F16 mistakenly also received approval to land in the same direction. Neither pilot saw the other due to the angle they were coming from, and they collided. Miraculously, the C130 was able to right itself. The F16, however, went out of control and the pilots had to eject. The F16 crashed and struck a parked aircraft. The ensuing fireball, debris, and exploding munitions engulfed the paratroopers training on the Green Ramp.

Our location prevented us from seeing the wall of fire coming our way. I only remember the expression of total disbelief in my jumpmaster's eyes when he yelled, "An airplane is crashing toward us!" Instinctively, I dropped to the ground as the jet's fuselage roared past me and a sheet of flame rolled over me. In the next instant the roar was replaced by the screams of those around me.

When I got up, I felt pain on the back of my hands and head. I knew my injuries weren't life threatening because I wasn't bleeding or on fire. The paratrooper next to me, however, had been thrown against a metal door and was bleeding profusely from his forehead. I used my jacket to stop the bleeding, kept talking to him, and tried to keep him from going into shock. At that point, I saw the destruction and carnage that surrounded me. I felt utterly helpless as I saw scores of paratroopers around me on fire or mortally injured from burns, blast, or airborne debris. Twenty-four were killed and more than one hundred injured. Later I learned that this was the worst training accident in the history of the division.

Eventually, I arrived at the hospital, where my wife, Stephanie, worked. I was placed in a makeshift treatment room, clearly a lower priority than the more seriously injured paratroopers. Many had burns covering up to ninety percent of their bodies or severe injuries from shrapnel.

I remember seeing Stephanie for the first time that day. When our eyes met, we could see mutual concern, coupled with relief. The unspoken encouragement I received from her eyes was over-whelming. She didn't have time to talk because she was busy carry-ing information from the hospital staff to the families of the victims.

I remained in the hospital at Fort Bragg for four days while they cleaned my wounds and evaluated me for further surgery and treatment. During this period, I experienced pain like I had never known. Twice daily I underwent wound debridement treatments. A therapist ran my hands under water and removed the burned tissue and dirt from my skin with a metal scraper. I forgot to take the pain medicine prior to the first treatment and thought I was going to pass out. I didn't forget to do that again.

Later, I was transferred with a number of the other paratroopers, to Brooke Army Medical Center in Texas. There I received skin grafts to the backs of both my hands. Then I remained in traction for several days with arms braced and suspended from my shoulders to my fingertips to keep me from damaging the new skin.

Finally, I was allowed to go home and after thirty days on convalescent leave I was back in harness. Later that summer, I took command of an airborne company.

Many asked me why I wasn't more upset or angry at the pilots or air traffic controllers for allowing this accident to occur. Certainly that is one response. What I took from that hellish experience, however, was something quite different. For me I chose to relearn what was truly important and reset my priorities.

I don't really know why I was on the Green Ramp that day, or why God chose to spare me when men to my left and right were killed. The fact that God spared me means that His purpose in my life has not yet been fulfilled. I do know I will continue to live a life built on these words of the Apostle Paul, "Forgetting what lies behind and reaching forward to what lies ahead, I press on toward the goal for the prize of the upward call of God in Christ Jesus" (Phil. 3:13-14 NASB).

(Used by permission of Command magazine, published by Officers' Christian Fellowship, Englewood, Colorado.)

BUTTERFLIES AND WAR

★

J.WALKER WINSLOW
US ARMY

He makes me to lie down in green pastures;
He leads me beside the still waters. He restores my soul (Ps. 23:2-3).

Several days ago, I was enjoying a beautiful morning on my patio. I had coffee on the table and my focus was upon the dainty hummingbirds jockeying for position at one of two feeders. Suddenly, a large Monarch butterfly floated down to a plant on my table. The strikingly vibrant yellow and red of its magnificent wings were artfully outlined in black. God's creature posed in perfect profile, as if waiting for applause.

While watching, I felt transported from this moment to a day thirty years earlier against the backdrop of war.

I hated being in Vietnam and especially being downed just outside of the now deserted city of Wey. Wey had been an energetic, vital city of almost 200,000 inhabitants. I remembered seeing politicians meeting in the streets, workers building new homes, and children playing games that only children can play. After a few years of war, Wey became a mere skeleton. No one talked in the streets—no workers, and certainly no sounds of children playing. Stucco walls remained without roofs, displaying row after row of pockmarked reminders of automatic weapons' fire.

My role in Vietnam was to fly as an intelligence officer. Our plane had experienced significant maintenance failures, so the crew chiefs were checking it over. I was of no use to the "maintenance boys," so I stayed out of their way and strolled down the road to find a little peace.

A grassy knoll afforded a bit of protection from the ominous jungle. I lay on my back and wondered if the sky was just as clear thousands of miles away, above my wife and two young sons. *God, I hate this war*, I thought.

I realized that I was staring into that vast blue void, trying to see the face of God. I was so angry.

Suddenly, a large, beautiful Monarch butterfly landed on a plant near where I lay. Its fragile beauty overwhelmed me. God's creature posed in perfect profile, and a deep sense of peace came over me.

I was in deep reverie when I heard the maintenance sergeant calling, "The bird's fixed, we can go. I think we'll be all right."

As I stood to return to the ship, the butterfly fluttered, paused, then flew over the knoll.

All that I could think of to say was, "You know, Sarge, I think you're right."

In Weakness, Strength

★

And He said to me, "My grace is sufficient for you,
for My strength is made perfect in weakness."
Therefore most gladly I will rather boast in my infirmities,
that the power of Christ may rest upon me (2 Cor. 12:9).

There is something about Christmas that appeals to me more every year. I feel a deep sense of contentment seeing my children arrive home for Christmas. It means a great deal to me that they want to be with us and enjoy the special celebration that Christians share. We all marvel that the great God of the universe would choose to become small and weak to show us the way home. Two Christmases ago, I learned about weakness in a surprising way.

Military life is full of a variety of unexpected stresses. Moving as we have—eighteen times in twenty-five years—has had its own set of stresses. Yet, I didn't feel any of this building in a particular way. I felt I adapted well to the changing environment, long hours, and frequent separations. That was particularly true for me as an air force flying squadron commander.

I remember sitting in my reclining chair covered with a warm blanket a week before Christmas. I was feeling out of sorts and thought a little sleep would bring about a quick recovery. I watched the fire before me with the Christmas tree decorated beside it. Gradually, I noticed that my body felt oddly different.

I had a hard time lifting my left arm and my face felt funny, as if the dentist had put half of it to sleep. I began to rub it to get feeling back into it. But then I noticed the top of my head on the left side was growing numb as well. Even my toes on the left foot weren't responding the way they should.

It wasn't long after that I found myself on my back in a hospital bed looking up at a grim faced doctor. Probing this and that and asking an endless array of questions, the doctor kept aggravating me until he was satisfied with the answers he got. I was admitted and taken to various places in the hospital for tests to figure out what happened.

I heard a nurse whispering, "He's so young for MS," and I began to feel even weaker hearing this. Finally, I was back in my room and alone with my thoughts. Inside I felt strangely peaceful. So what if I were ill? I had a wonderful wife and children and the Lord had seen me through some pretty dark days. Couldn't He see me through this as well?

The neurologist came into the room. She walked with a cane and I wondered what had happened to her. She confirmed that there was a possibility I had suffered a stroke, but that there was a possibility I was in the initial stages of multiple sclerosis. My wife sat beside me on the bed throughout this conversation. When the doctor left we sat quietly and held hands.

We had been married twenty plus years and I had a complete confidence many other married folks might not have. I knew, without a doubt, that Cindy would stay beside me in sickness and in health until the end. I can tell you that I have never been as grateful to God for my wife as I was at that moment. When I realized that I could soon be too weak even to feed myself, I was strengthened knowing that God was above me and my wife was beside me. All my years of flying jets around the world paled in comparison to that sure, sweet, and certain knowledge.

For three days, I stayed in that bed in the same condition. I drew close to the Lord and felt His sure presence. I didn't pray to God to heal me. I was confident He knew where I was, and I trusted Him to know the condition He wanted for me.

It was about midnight when I felt a strong presence of God in the room. In my heart I heard Him say, "I'm not finished with you yet." The sense of His closeness faded, but as I marveled at the sweetness of that moment, I felt a tingling in my hands and feet. My cheek felt different. Over the next few hours, I felt the strength returning to my hands, arms, and legs as the numbness disappeared.

In the early morning, I called the nurse and told her that I was well again. I didn't know how to express to the medical staff what had happened. They were completely shocked by the speed of my recovery. Physician after physician came through to examine me. I was well, and there was nothing they could say to deny it. Neither could they say I hadn't been ill. They were left without a suitable explanation. They chocked it up to a brain virus and closed the file.

As for me, I checked out of the hospital the next day to return to flying status. But my heart and faith had been taken to a new depth. I used to sing a song, "I am weak but He is strong." Since my illness and healing, I rejoice in my weakness because through it, I experienced His strength.

WHY ME?

★

MAJOR THADDEUS "TJ" JANKOWSKI
USMC RESERVES

The Spirit Himself bears witness with our spirit that we are children of God, and if children, then heirs—heirs of God and joint heirs with Christ, if indeed we suffer with Him, that we may also be glorified together (Rom. 8:16-17).

Did you ever ask the question, "Why me, Lord?" Maybe you were tempted to ask such a question, or at least feel a little sorry for yourself, when your physical or emotional endurance was tested. Perhaps such thoughts reared their head when you watched a friend or relative go through the fire. It certainly isn't uncommon to face such suppressed misgivings and doubts as I did one night while serving with a young marine in north central Honduras. One evening he took me aside and explained how his mother had suffered permanent brain damage in an automobile wreck. In the middle of the battalion compound, he shared his doubts and misgivings and asked, "Why?"

On a purely rational plane, he had a vague notion of the possibility that God might have a purpose he couldn't yet see. He wasn't bitter. His was a broken, searching soul looking for a lighthouse on a sturdy outcropping. He was looking for a place where he could cling and find answers to his questions.

What could I say to such a man? At the time, I hadn't experienced a comparable sorrow in my life. I couldn't speak from experience. So, with sensitive caution I shared about God's sovereignty, His goodness, His omniscience and power. I told him how God delights in bringing good out of evil, and how these kinds of experiences draw us closer to God.

What does it take for you to get mad at God—to shake your fist at the heavens and demand to know if anyone is listening, if anyone cares? I would soon get my chance to face my own personal moment of truth.

I had been a platoon commander at Camp Pendleton about six months when I awoke with a swelling in my neck. About a week before, I had completed a seventeen-mile forced march with pack and rifle. I was working my platoon up to twenty five-miles as part of our battalion's combat certification test.

I showed my neck to my company commander, then to the battalion surgeon, who sent me to the hospital. I didn't feel bad, but within twenty-four hours, doctors told me I had developed Hodgkin's disease. I was informed that it was a malignant cancer that was attacking my lymph system. I, a tough marine infantry officer, cried many tears. However, God had taken me a long way, as I watched others who came before me, experience their moment of crisis. By His grace, my tears were not in bitterness and anger. I felt no need to question His goodness, His timing, or His power. I fell on my knees often that first weekend in the hospital. I offered continual praise to God for counting me worthy to have served Him. When I say that, I am not boasting. Rather, I am testifying to His goodness toward me.

Every doctor asked me if I had experienced shortness of breath. They asked me this question, sometimes a second time, just to be sure of my answer. I finally asked them how large the tumors were that were in my chest. The doctor shocked me with his answer: "Your cancer takes up thirty percent of your chest cavity." I started chemotherapy immediately. That painful treatment lasted six months. I learned so much during that time.

A son might believe his mother's livelihood was snuffed out prematurely, but God still requires us to trust and obey. A young man, in the prime of life and at the beginning of his career, may awake to find his health and life hanging by a thread. Through God's ever-present grace, we can still trust Him.

Somehow, grateful hearts and praise from our lips please the Lord. It isn't until we approach the throne of God on the final day, that we will truly comprehend the words of Paul, ". . . the sufferings of this present time are not worthy to be compared with the glory which shall be revealed in us" (Rom. 8:18).

(Editor's note: TJ was diagnosed with cancer while a young officer on active duty in the Marine Corps. After six months of chemical and radiation therapy, he was able to return to duty and enjoys good health today).

(Used by permission of Command magazine, published by Officers' Christian Fellowship, Englewood, Colorado.)

PRAYERS FOR GUNNY

★

JIM "GUNNY" BOYLE
SGT. USMC

The earnest prayer of a righteous person has great power and wonderful results (James 5:16 NLT).

I want to begin by saying I had a praying grandmother, because without knowing that, you can't really understand my story. Her prayers and the prayers of my mother are the reason I'm alive today. She believed in me, even when I no longer believed in myself. She'd told me from the time I was five, "God has his hand on you, son, and I'm praying for you. Never forget, I'm praying for you."

Now, it wasn't that I didn't believe in God, because I did. However, I used prayer like an insurance policy. I kept it for a rainy day and brought it out only when I was in serious trouble. At the end of my first enlistment in the marines, I planned to get out of the service. However, my first daughter was born prematurely and placed in an incubator. They expected her to be in there for a full month. There was no way I could get out of the Marine Corps. So I prayed, "Lord, if You save my daughter, when I retire from the Marine Corps, I'll commit the rest of my life to serving You." Well, the Lord answered my prayer, and I quickly forgot my promise.

I lived the life of the stereotypical macho marine—hard-drinking, hard-loving lifestyle. When you're living like that, you don't stay the same, you keep sinking lower and lower.

Anyone who grew up in the 1960s knows that being in Vietnam was a distinctly unpleasant and unhealthy place to be. My first tour in Vietnam was in 1964 as part of an infantry battalion, off the coast of Da Nang. We were there to make amphibious landings when the orders came down. My second tour to Vietnam was in 1970 at Red Beach in Da Nang. God's protecting hand upon me during both tours kept me out of harm's way. But His protection certainly had nothing to do with my faith because then I didn't have much time for God.

Returning stateside from Vietnam, I was re-assigned to a unit at Camp Pendleton in California. While on leave following my tour overseas, I was informed the battalion I'd just been assigned to was being sent back over to Vietnam.

I was going through a divorce at the time, so I asked the Marine Corps for a humanitarian transfer until I could finish with the legalities involved. Then I would rejoin my unit. The Marine Corps was not impressed by my request. I got a telegram from headquarters saying my request did not meet the requisites for humanitarian transfer. The entire first page explained why I wasn't entitled to this treatment. I turned the page and the first word was "However." It went on to say a position had been found for me and I was detached from my current unit. As a result, I did not get shipped back over to Vietnam, and I can tell you that this was a very significant event. Shortly after my unit arrived in-country it made a very large-scale amphibious landing. The entire battalion sustained massive casualties. God had His hand on me, but I didn't know it yet. Meanwhile, Grandma kept praying.

A couple of years later, as I was getting ready to retire, everything in my life fell apart. I was drinking heavily, my second wife divorced me, and about this time my youngest daughter became seriously ill. She was in the hospital in Hawaii, diagnosed with leukemia. As the days became weeks, she grew increasingly weak and was transferred to the intensive care unit. Our family stayed at her bedside around the clock.

She was such a sweet child and loved the Lord with all her heart. She also loved *Voyage of the Dawn Treader*, book three of *The Chronicles of Narnia*. In the story, the children sail into the sea of darkness, also known as the sea of death. At about that time, as I read, my daughter starting patting my hand. I looked over at her and asked, "Is everything all right, honey?"

"Everything's fine now, Dad" she said. She looked at me and smiled. Then she closed her eyes and died.

For the next three nights I couldn't sleep. In my grief, I kept hear-

ing the words, "Finish the book, finish the book, finish the book."
Finally, I did. At the end of the story, the children come out of the sea
of death into a beautiful, calm sea of glass. The children rowed their
boat ashore and were met by a lamb cooking fish over a fire. As the
children approached the lamb, he changed into the Christ figure of
the story, Aslan the lion.

At that moment, the message shot into my heart. My daughter
was with the Lord and she was okay. In my relief and grief, I began
to reflect on my life in a way I'd never done before.

After all those years, I was finally at the bottom. I had lost my
marriage; I had lost the love of my sweet daughter; and I'd retired
from the Marine Corps. I went into a very deep depression and
needed to talk to someone. A Christian couple I'd known for some
time met with me. The moment the woman saw me she said, "You're
not looking too good today, Bill. Is something wrong?"

That question unleashed a flood of emotions that just overwhelmed me. All I could say was "Nobody loves me." Well, she looked
me straight in the eye and said three words that changed my life:
"Jesus loves you."

When she said that I started bawling like a baby. This big old
macho marine just lost it. That day, I prayed to receive His love and
it has changed my life.

My grandmother told me that I'd be a minister someday and,
though she didn't live to see it, it did happen. One day soon, I'll sail
into the sea of death and come out the other side where the Lamb,
my grandmother, and my daughter will greet me. On that wonderful day I'll start by praising the Lamb, Jesus. Then I'm going to hug
my daughter and thank my grandmother—the grandmother who
believed in me and kept reminding me until she died, "Never forget.
I'm praying for you."

A TIME FOR HEROES (PART 2)

★

SWIFT, SILENT, AND DEADLY—

MARINE RECON AND MY LAST PATROL

CLEBE MCCLARY

1ST LT., USMC

And we know that all things work together for good to those who love God, to those who are the called according to His purpose (Rom. 8:28).

It was in the autumn of 1967 when I arrived in the Republic of Vietnam. Only a few short months before, I had been newly wed and newly commissioned as a second lieutenant. It was difficult leaving behind a loving family and what I considered a marriage made in heaven to my wife Deanna. But I was eager for action and proud to serve my country in the Marine Corps.

When our Braniff jet touched down on the tarmac at Da Nang, military activity was picking up, particularly in the northernmost section of the country where I would be assigned.

I was directed to the First Marine Division's First Reconnaissance Battalion five miles from Da Nang. In short order, we new arrivals were debriefed and assigned by the general in charge of marine operations in I Corps. During the debriefing, he asked if any of us wanted to volunteer for "recon" duty. Recon (short for reconnaissance) was a known synonym for suicide. This unit, which I considered the Marine Corps' best, operated covertly behind enemy lines. It was made up of a small team of men playing a dangerous game of hide-and-seek with the enemy. In spite of the memories of my wife's pleas to stay out of recon, I jumped at the chance. After a few warm-up patrols, I was given command of my first platoon.

We worked the territory within a forty-five-mile radius of the base and became a thorn in the enemy's side. We had to go no farther than the first hill to fight. Helicopters transported us to and from our assignments in the mountains and jungles where we would spend from four to twenty-six days conducting reconnaissance and surveillance operations. Our primary missions were detecting enemy troop movement and arms infiltration efforts as well as gathering information on the enemy's strength, position, and actions.

Some patrols were little more than a leisurely walk in the woods. Many of our forays, however, were close calls, leaving us a heartbeat from death. I found that recon teams either completed their mission safely or were badly mauled, with seldom a middle ground. Confrontations with the enemy occurred with horrific results. We killed only when we had to and avoided contact whenever possible.

As patrol leader, I usually took a twelve-man team into the bush. We became known as "Texas Pete and the Dirty Dozen." Behind enemy lines we were hunters, stalking a deadly prey. We chased him through impenetrable jungle, hacking our way through and across mile-high mountains. We lugged 110-pound packs on our backs, sometimes pulling them behind us through vegetation so thick we had to crawl. Using movement as a defensive tactic, we snooped and hid making it hard for Charlie to find us.

I constantly tried to imagine what Charlie would do if he were in my place and then did something else. When we had to fight, we usually hit and ran. We neither picked fights nor dodged them. A fire-fight was sort of like a ball game: whoever shot the most the fastest won, and whoever got off the first shot lived. A skirmish didn't bother me at the time, but I was a little shaken afterward when I had time to think about what might have happened.

As a chameleon changes colors to blend with his surroundings, we painstakingly camouflaged ourselves to blend with jungle greens and browns. While we smeared our faces with camouflage makeup sticks, Pfc. Ralph Johnson, a good-natured black marine from Charleston, South Carolina, grumbled, "Lieutenant, I'm black enough! Why have I gotta put that stuff on me?" It was necessary to dull the shine of the skin. We didn't wear rings that could sparkle in the sun, and even my Marine Corps watch had a black face and band.

Anything that rattled had to be taped down. We found that helmets and flight jackets made too much noise in the jungle. A bandanna with leaves stuck in it or a canvas camouflage hat served better. All supplies were painted brown, green, and black.

Charlie was also a master of camouflage. Waiting for us to come by, the VC sometimes buried themselves for forty-eight hours straight, breathing fresh air through a straw. Other times they sat covered in a hole called a "spider trap" for weeks with only a handful of rice to eat each day.

Trails and roads were rarely used. Instead, we followed animal paths or cut our way through the vines and sometimes traveled in rivers and streams. Movement was often slow; some days we traveled several miles and other days only a few hundred yards.

The order of march placed the point man first to scout for mines and booby traps. He usually carried both an M-79 (grenade launcher) and M-14 (assault rifle), effective at long range. We changed the point man about every two hours because if he became fatigued and careless, we could be killed. It happened to others. My position was second, the primary radio man behind me, followed by the "Doc" (Navy corpsman), an M 16 rifleman, an auxiliary radio man, and finally, "tail-end Charlie." His job was to cover our trail by smoothing footprints and pulling vines and leaves over our path. If he suspected we were being followed, he set out booby traps and Claymore mines.

Walking single file, we were careful not to step on the same rock as any other man in the team. Otherwise, the fourth or fifth man would kick it loose and slide down the hill making noise, or possibly suffering injury. If we heard anything, everyone froze. Thumbs down signaled that it was the enemy. Coming to a bomb crater, open place, or stream, we stopped and let the first man cover the second man, and so on, until we all passed safely. When we made noise by hacking vines or cutting trees, we froze and waited to see if Charlie heard and was making a move to reach us. Even putting a poncho on in rainy weather became an art simply because the slightest rustle might give our position away.

Settling into our camp before dark, we placed Claymore mines, booby traps, and trip flares around our position to give us ample warning if Charlie hit. On occasion, he disconnected our mines and slipped to within a few feet of us to leave Communist propaganda for harassment. He was that good.

Darkness was our disadvantage, and Charlie knew it. He usually hit around midnight or just before daybreak. Many times throughout the night, we ordered H&I (High Explosive and Incendiary) fire from artillery around our position. These intermittent artillery barrages not only made the enemy a little leery of coming too close to us, but also kept artillery warmed up and hitting on target if we needed it to counter an enemy assault. We avoided movement at night—not even visits to the privy were allowed. We took turns sleeping, but often we were on 100 percent alert: everybody awake. We formed a 360-degree circle with a string running from my leg to each other man's leg. Lying on the ground beneath the stars, we made friends with the jungle creatures. By morning, the birds and monkeys thought we were one of them and had adjusted to our presence.

As we chased Charlie, we waged small-scale warfare against our other enemies—insects, heat, and disease. Leeches attached themselves to the waist, wrists, and ankles unless we tucked in shirts, tied our pants at the ankles and our sleeves at the wrists. As temperatures soared, we took salt tablets almost daily. On Sunday, we took our yellow malaria pills to ward off the fever. In addition, we received routine shots to combat disease in the tropical climate.

Because there were many teams sent into the bush, my team rarely received as much ammo as requested. There was sufficient ammo for the teams to have a mediocre supply, but if one team took everything it wanted, another team would be weakened.

My troops were tough. Their performance was superior and their morale was outstanding, despite the anti-war sentiment at home. They obeyed patrol orders almost to the letter and pulled us through some life-or-death encounters. I watched teenagers molded into men by the harsh realities of war. The medals they won were earned by gallantry—not the eloquence of the poet's eulogy, but the pain and anguish of blood sacrifice. Some men in my outfit had protested and demonstrated against the war while in college. When they came face to face with the Communist threat in Vietnam, they saw it differently—as a struggle for freedom.

As the months passed, recon was covering twice the area with half as many teams as when I arrived in Vietnam. Half of the men had been sent north as activity there intensified.

The news reports of ominous scenes in Southeast Asia increasingly troubled those back home. Immense anxiety showed in letters I received from Mom and Dad in early January, 1968, "We continue to pray and worry from one letter to the next. The news on the TV and radio and in the papers seems worse every day. Please use every precaution."

There is a verse in the Bible that says, "So don't worry about tomorrow, for tomorrow will bring its own worries. Today's trouble is enough for today" (Matt. 6:34, NLT). That's the way I lived in 'Nam, one day at a time. I didn't worry about the threat of tomorrow; I simply focused on doing my job to the best of my ability and entrusting my safety to the Lord.

More than once I sensed God guiding me and my men. When our choppers safely straddled mines that should have blown us away, I knew we were in divine custody. Family and friends, even churches bombarded heaven with prayers for my safekeeping.

As the war ground on, the battle activity accelerated. A truce for the Vietnamese observance of Tet—the Buddhist New Year—was like an intermission in a war movie. It was time to catch our breath. My platoon received permission to take gifts to Vietnamese families in Phuoc Ly Hoa Min, a village of 232 in Hoa Van District, Quang Nam Province. The village chief had me at his table for hot tea, rice bread, and cookies while my men were served rice wine and Tiger beer. This pleasant interlude was just the calm before the coming storm. In early '68, all hell broke loose. The enemy launched a major counteroffensive during Tet, hitting all of the major cities in South Vietnam except Da Nang.

I had been in Vietnam for five months at that time. In a few days, I would be on an R & R flight to Hawaii to meet my wife. It would be ten days short of a year since we had been married back at Quantico. I had already completed eighteen hazardous recon patrols deep into enemy territory without serious injury, and I had one last patrol to pull before my reunion with Deanna. After R & R, I expected to be promoted to company commander. I had delayed R & R until I could tell Dea that my bush fighting was behind me. I was saving this good news for the celebration of our first anniversary in Hawaii.

I had no dark premonitions about the mission to Hill 146, a stationary combat observation post deep in enemy-controlled territory. In five months as patrol leader, I hadn't lost a man and I didn't expect to this time.

My thirteen-man team included some veteran troops: Private First Class Ralph Johnson, Private First Class Tom Jennings, Private First Class Rod Hunter, and Captain Bob Lucas. Most of the other men were new, including Lance Corporal Thomas L. Jones, Private First Class H.G. "Henry" Covarrubias, Private First Class Burkhart, and Navy Corpsman Shawn Green. Most of my regulars had left the bush for office assignments.

Hill 146 measured roughly seventy-five meters from east to west and fifty meters from north to south. As our chopper hovered in a cleared area for us to jump out, the propellers stirred up dirt that had concealed three box mines. Jennings hit the deck and cut the wires to the mines. My radio man and corpsman dug a foxhole to my left, and three other men took cover in a foxhole to my right; the remaining eight were at the western end about fifty yards behind me around the perimeter of a bomb crater which was about twenty feet deep. We were in an excellent position to fight. I felt a nagging uneasiness as we guessed the enemy was up to something, something big. Through two tense days and nights, we watched and waited. An ominous intuition began to build that we were going to get hit.

The silence of the third day warned us to get ready. We were aware of the NVA's (North Vietnamese Army) ability to move silently through even the most rugged terrain. Usually, they knew the exact shape of the position they intended to attack and where the patrol leader would be. The hill was terraced into what was almost a stairway up the sides.

I got a call from a friend on duty that night asking how we were doing. I told him that enemy rockets and mortars indicated we were in for a long night. Reminding me that we were to meet our wives in Hawaii in a few days, he cautioned, "Take care, Clebe."

The darkness settled heavy with foreboding. We looked, listened, and waited. It was just after midnight, March 3, 1968 when the enemy hit. It was also my wife's birthday.

The men to my right cried out as a grenade fell into their foxhole. Johnson jumped on it, smothering it with his stomach to protect his two buddies. He died immediately.[10] One of the pair in the bomb crater, Jennings, was struck by shrapnel. The small wound apparently severed an artery, causing him to bleed profusely. Seven others, including our corpsman and our radioman, were wounded in the initial assault. My whole team was about to be overrun. I moved from one position to another, directing our desperate defense.

By this time, my left hand had been blown off by a fragmentation grenade.

Another grenade came in. I saw it in time to throw up my right hand to protect my face. The pain shot through me as if an ax had split my head! My left eye was torn out, the vision in my right eye blurred by blood. The blast had burst both eardrums and mutilated my right hand.

I remember thinking, "If I can just reach the safety of the bomb crater . . ." when another grenade shredded my legs with hot shrapnel.

Death looked me over—a helpless heap of bleeding flesh and splintered bones. PFC Hunter ("Chief" as we called him) had bolted from the bomb crater to search for me when he saw an NVA ready to shoot me in the head. Instead, Chief shot him first, causing the enemy's bullet to pierce my arm.

"Lieutenant! Lieutenant!"

"Chief! Is that you?" I gasped.

"Yes, sir!" Chief said. Kneeling by my feet, he began picking off the enemy as they charged up the hill. Having saved my life once, he remained at my side returning enemy fire while I lay near death.

I told Lucas to take over the patrol and call in the choppers to pick us up. He radioed the pilots who told him they couldn't come until daylight because of the rain and fog. "Forget it!" he told them. "Nobody will be left at daylight!"

Though I had requested ten, we had been issued only five grenades per man. In no time, they were used up. My men then lobbed rocks down the side of the hill, hoping the enemy would think they were grenades and pull back.

The chopper pilots reconsidered and decided to come in immediately. Meanwhile, we called in two "Spooky" units. These were World War II, night-capable aircraft, equipped with Vulcan guns harnessing enough firepower to kick up dirt every square foot for one hundred yards. They were reserved for whoever was getting hurt the worst. I had requested them on other occasions but never got them. That night I got two. They could have been on the other side of the country, but the Lord sent them to us. Their red tongues of tracer fire were the only things that kept up our morale while we waited for the choppers to come in.

If the NVA had followed up their initial assault, we would have been wiped out. Attacking from three sides—north, east, and south—they had avoided the western side where our machine guns were set up. Thus, it became impossible for us to fire the M-60s in the direction of their assault without hitting our own men.

Creeping silently to within fifteen to twenty yards of our position without being detected, the enemy had disconnected all our mines and booby traps. With ten of our thirteen men dead or wounded, we would have been an easy conquest if they had followed through. It must have taken a while for them to reorganize at the bottom of the hill. Whatever the reason, it helped save our lives by buying us precious time.

"Doc" Green regained consciousness and began fighting to save my life. My pulse rate was thirty-six beats per minute (the average is seventy-five). Had my heart beat at a normal rate, I could have bled to death. My left arm, severed just below the elbow, did not bleed as much as it would have if amputated about the joint. The arteries appeared to have been seared shut by the hot metal from the grenade. Doc put a tourniquet on the stump of my arm and started to tie off my left leg, which was shredded like hamburger. Knowing that I would lose it for sure if a tourniquet was applied, I kicked him away. Because I had sustained head wounds, morphine could not be administered for pain.

The first chopper landed at our position about 1 a.m. and was immediately loaded with wounded, dead, and dying. The rest of the men piled into the second chopper, all except Chief Hunter and me. The chopper crew thought I was dead and urged him to leave me behind. He ignored their pleas and risked his own life to save mine a second time. Grabbing me under the arms, Chief dragged me fifty yards to the chopper, lifted me aboard, and held me with my legs dangling out as the helicopter took off. Immediately, some 150 NVA stormed the hill in force. A delay of just minutes and not one of us would have left that hill alive.

The pain from the wounds and cold air proved almost unbearable by the time we landed twenty minutes later at Marble Mountain Hospital near Da Nang. Attendants hustled me onto a stretcher and began cutting away my blood-drenched clothes. "Don't cut my boots! They'll be ruined!" I objected feebly. They snipped them anyway as I'd seen them do to dying troopers before, while the doctors and corpsmen started cursing and slapping me. *Why did they bring me this far to beat me to death?* I wondered.

Aching and angry, I tried to strike back. The tactic worked. Most of my veins had collapsed from loss of blood, but the slapping and cursing made me respond, reviving a vein in the temple. I felt the prick of a small needle, and as the life-sustaining blood began to flow, I mercifully lost consciousness.

Jennings died half an hour after reaching the hospital. Burkhart, suffering multiple shrapnel wounds, was med-evaced out of the country. Five others were treated for minor shrapnel wounds and released.

For days I lingered closer to death than life. I was vaguely aware of a frantic effort to keep me alive. Tubes protruded from my torn body like hoses from a car engine. My pain was equal to a taste of hell.

Before they med-evaced me out of the country, the men of my platoon paraded by, one at a time, for a last look. Lieutenant Barta cried like a baby. "Top" Barker refused to come. He said he wanted to remember me the way I was because I was the only lieutenant he ever knew "worth a cuss."

While I was fighting for my life, my wife's joyous expectations of meeting me in Hawaii were suddenly shattered by the delivery of one of those ominous telegrams from the Commandant of the U.S. Marine Corps. It read:

A REPORT RECEIVED THIS HEADQUARTERS REVEALS THAT YOUR HUSBAND SECOND LIEUTENANT PATRICK C MCCLARY III USMC SUSTAINED INJURIES ON 3 MARCH 1968 IN THE VICINITY OF QUANG NAM REPUBLIC OF VIETNAM FROM A HOSTILE GRENADE WHILE ON A PATROL. HE SUFFERED TRAUMATIC AMPUTATION TO THE LEFT ARM AND SUSTAINED SHRAPNEL WOUNDS TO ALL EXTREMITIES. PROGNOSIS IS POOR. OUTLOOK DIM. YOUR GREAT ANXIETY IS UNDERSTOOD AND YOU ARE ASSURED THAT HE WILL RECEIVE THE BEST OF CARE. YOU SHALL BE KEPT INFORMED OF ALL SIGNIFICANT CHANGES IN HIS CONDITION.

I finally arrived by med-evac flight at the U.S. Army 249th General Hospital at Camp Drake, Japan. I was in critical condition and not much to look at. Where my left arm had been, there was now just a stump. The grenade explosion had torn out my left eye. My right hand was mangled by the blast when I tried to shield my face. My right leg was full of shrapnel, the left one shredded, gangrenous, and my feet were black from jungle rot. Besides the physical torture, the mental anguish over my condition, the mounting concerns from my loved ones back home, my inability to adequately console them was unbearable.

However, as I gradually regained my strength, I found myself able to thank God for the fact that I was still alive. I hurt, but I was not a bitter, broken man. All I wanted was to go home. The flood of condolences and words of encouragement poured in, but I desperately needed to see my wife and family and begin to pick up the pieces. By the end of March, arrangements were finally made for me to be transferred to Bethesda Naval Hospital in Maryland.

As the days passed, however, my emotional condition took a turn for the worse. I knew enough about God not to question His ways. But I could not imagine what purpose He had in my experiences. I tried to sound convincing as I encouraged Dea on a tape that I sent. Still I would look at my arm, think about my eye, and wonder.

Inevitably, the time arrived when I asked, "Why me, Lord?" Taking a good look at myself and remembering how beautiful Deanna was, I began to think she would be better off without me. I became so depressed that I gave up. I lost my desire to live. People used to tease me by asking good-naturedly what a beautiful girl like Dea was doing with somebody like me. I would quip, "It's my personality and Southern charm!" But suddenly it wasn't funny anymore. I lost hope and wished I could die.

It was at that moment when a heaven-sent visitor walked onto the ward. My temperature was 108 degrees and I had no fight left. He stopped by one bed and then another. He had a deck of playing cards in his hand with his photograph on each card. He'd say something to each man and then leave them a card. As he neared my bed, the doctor told him, "Don't bother with him, he isn't going to make it."

He walked up to my bed anyway and put a playing card under my pillow. Though I was in bad condition, I could see and hear him. He put his hand on my shoulder and said, "Thank you for what you did. I'm praying for you and I love you." That was just what I needed. That man gave me the will to fight on. His name was Billy Caspar and he went on to win the 1969 Masters Golf Tournament. God sent an encouraging word to me just when I needed it.

After an agonizing month of waiting, I made the long med-evac flight home to be reunited with my wife. As she entered my hospital ward for the first time, my words to her were "Dea, honey, it's me. Baby, I know I'm not a pretty sight, but I'm happy to be alive and home."

There I lay, a pathetic 115 pounds, with bandages covering the left eye and both ears. My head was shaved, face full of stitches. I had the stump of my left arm bound and my right arm in a cast and motionless. My left leg was open and draining with the bone exposed, and the right leg covered with shrapnel wounds.

"You're beautiful!" she cried. Running to me, she gently wrapped her arms around my frail form, afraid of hurting me. "Don't worry," she assured me. "We're going to make the best of everything."

Several operations followed to remove metal from my head, gums, forearm, legs, and feet. One eardrum was reconstructed, using the lining of a vein in my temple. The other eardrum was rebuilt in later surgery at Philadelphia Naval Hospital. After the reconstructive surgery, my hearing greatly improved. Most of my teeth had to be capped. Surgery was also performed on my left eye to remove the damaged tissue. I received an artificial eye but eventually adopted a black patch instead.

All my plans for a promising military career had been blown to bits that night on Hill 146, and I didn't know what the future held. I was pretty sure that it would be a long road back to what I considered a normal life. Reconstructing something meaningful out of the ashes of what had been wasn't easy. It had all the built-in fears and insecurities one would expect of someone in my condition. But things would not turn out as I anticipated; God had other, long-range plans for my life.

When the smoke of battle clears, the bodies are buried, and the peace treaty is signed that's when the rebuilding begins. For me, the war was over. The challenge facing me was to rebuild a devastated life. Little did I know at the time that God wanted to cooperate.

During my first leave from the hospital in Florence, South Carolina (Dea's hometown), an evangelistic crusade was being held at the football stadium where I had thrown and caught a couple of touchdown passes and played many games. I read in the newspaper that Bobby Richardson, former second baseman with the New York Yankees, and Vonda Kay Van Dyke, former Miss America from Arizona, were to participate. While coaching in Florence, I had once invited Bobby to speak at my school. I said to Deanna, "I'd sure like to see Bobby Richardson," and of course, any Marine would like to see Miss

America! So we went to the stadium on the night of July 26, 1968.

We heard Bobby and Vonda Kay give brief testimonies, sharing what the Lord Jesus Christ had done in their lives. Then came the message that God used to change my life. Billy Zeoli, president of Gospel Communications, preached to us about some of the great men of the Bible who had become "fools for God." He spoke of Noah, who likely was labeled a fool by the people in his community when he built an ark at God's command. He told of Joshua, who must have been ridiculed by his soldiers when he announced God's battle plans for Jericho. He mentioned others who obeyed God, though it seemed foolish to men. He said that if they were fools, they were fools for God. He said there are two kinds of fools in this world. fools for Christ and fools for others. The greatest fool of all, he added, is one who hears God's plan of salvation and rejects it. "Whose fool are you?" he asked. "Whose fool are you?" Those words dug into my soul like red-hot slivers of shrapnel.

His question seemed to slap me in the face. I realized whose fool I'd been all of my life. In order to become a good athlete and to impress people I never drank or smoked. I was a good person, playing the role people expected of me. I grew up in church and believed in the right things—the Bible, tithing, good morals, and clean habits—but I had never invited Jesus Christ into my heart as Savior or let Him become the Lord of my life.

When the invitation was given, I stood. To my left, Dea also stood. With my left eye gone and hearing poor in the left ear, I was not aware that God had touched us both until we walked forward together to receive Christ as our personal Savior. We had difficulty finding someone to counsel with us; everyone thought we were Christians who had come to assist with the counseling!

My heart was changed that midsummer's night, but my life did not change noticeably. For years, I had tried to live the Christian life; the difference was that now Christ was living in me. When this marine surrendered to the Lord, it was not defeat but rather victory. In the Marine Corps I had sought only to serve my country. As a new believer, I joined a greater army—the army of Jesus Christ.

God's purpose became clear: He spared my life that I might find abundant life in Him. I did not know it at the time, but through my experiences, He was to touch countless lives.

Months of painful therapy followed, but it involved more than just physical recovery. God began to adjust the steps of my life and direct them into His service. He planned to redeem my experiences in Vietnam for the benefit of others. Opportunity after opportunity presented itself to share my testimony and the life-changing power of Christ. Finally, in September of 1973, I felt the Lord leading me into full-time evangelism. After much prayer, Dea and I organized the Clebe McClary Evangelistic Association. We have witnessed in churches, evangelistic crusades, civic organizations, prisons, and over five hundred high schools.

The nightmare of Vietnam is not easily forgotten. The horrors of that midnight on Hill 146 will never be erased. Daily my wife and I are reminded of the high cost of liberty by the price that I paid—100 percent disability.

But even saddled with such a discouraging label, we have found it exciting to look ahead and see what can still be achieved. We are not bitter or angry, but grateful in the profound revelation that though I paid a heavy price in flesh and blood, Christ paid a far greater price by laying down His life for me. It was a reality that I was forced to appreciate that desperate night on Hill 146 when Ralph Johnson gave his life to save his two buddies. It is with this recognition that I have dedicated my life to His service.

Together, my wife and I are living testimonies of the power of Christ to bring good out of bad and meaning out of meaninglessness. As the great assurance of Romans 8:28 declares, He has caused it all to work together for good—not only for our lives but for many who have learned of God's love through His work in my life.

(This story was originally published in *Vietnam: The Other Side of Glory* by William Kimball, was updated following a recent interview with Clebe McClary by the author. He may be contacted at PO Box 535 Pawleys Island South Carolina 29585 (843) 237-2582.)

A Time
to Lead

Leaders are people who do the right thing; managers are people who do things right. Both roles are crucial, but they differ profoundly. I often observe people in top positions doing the wrong thing well.

Warren Bennis

A leader does not deserve the name unless he is willing occasionally to stand alone.

Henry Kissinger

Be the chief but never the lord.

Lao-Tzu

You learn to know a pilot in a storm.

Seneca the younger

TOUGH AND TENDER — A GODLY PORTRAIT OF LEADERSHIP

★

MAJ. GEN. JOE GRAY (RETIRED)
US ARMY

Light arises in the darkness for the upright;
He is gracious and compassionate and righteous. Psalm 112: 4 (NASB)

As a major general in the army in the early 1980s, I was asked to go on a talk show. Usually that's considered a pretty high-threat environment. The theme of the talk show that day was leadership challenges of senior officers. The woman who was moderating the show caught me a little off-guard when she asked, "How, as a commander, can you still be tough while being tender at the same time?"

That was a great question, and a difficult one for someone who has been a commander seven times. I was never one to exhibit my feelings. Consequently, I came across as a pretty demanding leader. Yet, inside I cared and was always concerned for the men and women who served with me.

As a leader, there are areas in which you cannot compromise. At the same time, while using sound judgment, you want to be compassionate and fair. I was dedicated to our mission to ensure the highest standards of training and readiness. But I also cared about the soldiers who carried out our training mission. As I thought about that question, I reflected back to an event that took place some twenty years earlier, when I was a first lieutenant.

I had been company commander of the Fourteenth Battalion, Third Regiment for about a year. We were a basic unit training company for infantrymen, preparing them to join their first operational unit. We kept the men very busy and there was little time for relaxation. The 1960s demanded that we produce men who were trained and ready for whatever they were going to face in southeast Asia or elsewhere.

I was a young, enthusiastic officer, fully committed to my unit and mission. Yet, having been an enlisted soldier myself, I understood some of the problems the men faced. It came as somewhat of a surprise then, when I got word that one of the men was planning to go AWOL. I had my first sergeant bring the soldier in question in to talk with me.

It was starting to get cold in South Carolina as fall withered before the coming winter. My office was in the back of an old wooden army barracks, barely heated by a coal-fired stove. Dan[8] came into my small office and I invited him to sit on the wooden chair. He was nervous, and I tried to put him at ease. Dan had never given me any reason to worry about his performance until now.

"Dan, I think we may have a problem. Do you want to tell me what's bothering you?"

Dan looked down at the ground and kept silent.

"Dan, I can't help you unless you talk to me."

"I need to go home," he said quietly.

"Okay, help me understand. Why do you need to go home now?"

Again, he hesitated and then, slowly over the next half hour, the story came out. He had tears in his eyes.

"I'm not trying to get out of the army, and I'm not trying get out of work. But I've got to get home to take care of my brother and sister."

Dan had come from a very poor family in rural Mississippi. His dad had died and his mom couldn't afford to raise the two children. In her despair, she abandoned the children and left them alone in the cabin. They had no food, electricity, or running water.

"Sir, I joined the army to try to get money to take care of my mom and sister and brother. Now, my mom's run off and my brother and sister are alone."

He began to sob. "It's my responsibility. I'm the oldest one now."

He had a letter from home written by his sister. In it she begged for his help. Dan was an E-3 and had been sending home all of his pay. Even with that, his siblings had run out of fuel to heat the cabin and hadn't eaten for two days. Dan was afraid that if the social services folks heard of it, they'd take his sister and brother and break up their family.

"Sir, I've just got to hold my family together."

Well, there it was. The story had come out and now I was a part of it. As a training company, we didn't allow the troops leave during their final stages of unit training. If they didn't complete their training, they couldn't move on with their unit. Yet, this was a problem that cried out for a better answer than, *"Sorry, you can't have leave. Someone else will have to take care of your family."*

"Dan, I can't allow you to leave at this time. However, we're going to get you some help, starting right now."

And then our company went into action. We sent him over to the chaplain's office with the first sergeant while the officers and NCOs began to organize relief. The company pulled together and began to raise funds to help his family. We also got the Red Cross involved and they sent help as well. A foster family was arranged for Dan's siblings until he could get home to solve the problem. Here was a young man trying to be a brother and father at the same time. The least we could do was give a helping hand. Many members of the company prayed for Dan and his siblings, which served to draw our unit closer together.

In the end, Dan was able to finish his training and be reunited with his siblings in Mississippi. He was the kind of soldier that made you proud to be part of our army. Self-sacrifice came as naturally to him as breathing did to other folks. I was glad to play a small part in helping him out. A good soldier was saved, and I often wondered, during those Vietnam years, what happened to him and his family.

The mission of the military is accomplished with people, not machines. If we are going to be a strong fighting force, we've got to understand our people as well as we understand the equipment we're issued and the machines we operate. I believe that means listening to the heart of God when we make decisions about the lives of men and women. In doing so, I believe we will be both effective commanders and godly leaders.

And, in the end, isn't that a balance worth striving for? I think a soldier named Dan thought so. I know that the men and women who serve with and for you will think so too.

PRE-TAKEOFF CONFRONTATION

★

Who has woe? Who has sorrow? Who has contentions? Who has complaints? Who has wounds without cause? Who has redness of eyes? Those that linger long at the wine . . . (Prov. 23:29-30).

Twelve hours from bottle to throttle is an old axiom all pilots live by. More than just the pilots, all aircrew who control various aspects of the aircraft must abide by this rule. The military has a pretty strong tradition of working hard and playing hard, and certainly my unit was no different.

I was called in on a Sunday afternoon and told to recall all unit forces. My squadron of RC-135s was going to deploy within twenty-four hours to Okinawa, Japan. A crisis between China and Taiwan was brewing, and it looked like missiles were going to fly. Since we were stationed in the middle of the United States, I had preparations to make before starting the arduous seventeen-hour flight. I would assume command of this deployment of aircraft, fifty aircrew, and about one hundred maintenance crew members.

We arrived in Japan on schedule and our first sortie lifted off only a few hours later. From that point on we conducted round-the-clock flight operations for the next two weeks. We were there to observe and collect reconnaissance data on the events as they transpired. The crews were up to the grueling flights of twelve hours each, day after day. When the storm passed and the sides began to de-escalate, we all breathed a sigh of relief. We would be going home.

Because Japan was a fair distance from home, I had our flight crews stop off at Hickam AFB, Hawaii, on our way back to the states. I wanted to conduct further training from this location to prepare for future operations. Upon landing, our crews were released to enjoy some well-earned R&R. For me, this would be no vacation. I had to prepare for flight operations the next morning and ensure all was ready for the first sortie at 8:00 a.m.

It was just after dusk when I wandered down the street to a fast food restaurant to get something to eat. As I opened the door to leave, I stopped in stunned silence. There on the sidewalk to my left was a bag lady drinking from a brown paper bag. Next to her was a young man also drinking from a brown paper bag. I immediately recognized him. He was the pilot scheduled for the first morning flight out of Hickam!

I went back into the restaurant and gathered my thoughts. Was he really the pilot I thought he was? Yes, he was. Was it really within twelve hours of flight? I looked at my watch again; Yes, it was. Was he really drinking? I turned and watched him sip from the brown paper bag. Sadly, again the answer was yes. Not much I could do at this point but go out and deal with it.

I walked out and sat next to him on the sidewalk. He looked at me and turned red. He slowly moved the brown paper bag to his side and out of my sight. The bag lady got up and wandered away.

"So what's up?" I said

"Not much, " he replied quietly. "Just relaxing."

"You know we've got an early show time for the flight tomorrow?"

"Yes, sir," he said. "I'll be there."

I said, "Okay, we'll see you in the morning."

I got up and walked away. No point in making a scene on the street at that point. I had seen what I needed to and had enough facts to make a decision.

When I reported to the flight operations room in the morning I saw the operations officer. I told him to remove that pilot from the flight roster. He was shocked when I told him why.

It didn't take more than fifteen minutes for the pilot in question to find me. Though he was a captain and I was a lieutenant colonel, he lost his bearing and got right in my face.

"What do you mean taking me off the flight? You didn't see me drinking last night!" he said heatedly.

Now that was interesting. He didn't say, "I wasn't drinking," but rather, "You didn't see me drinking." This was definitely a young man in trouble. Moreover, I wanted to find a way of solving the problem without further embarrassing him. Conducting myself as a Christian should, whatever the situation, was important to me. I didn't always succeed, that's for sure. But it was a goal I strived toward.

I turned to him and said, "Now you'd better back off. Before I sat down on the sidewalk with you last night I watched you drink from the bottle. And now you're making me angry because you're lying to me. So back off!"

I turned and walked away, leaving him with his thoughts. I organized the pre-flight briefing and got the crews on their way to the aircraft. Once the aircraft were safely airborne, I returned to the hangar. It had been about two hours since our confrontation, and I was surprised to find a repentant young captain waiting for me.

"I'm meeting my promotion board next year. I've got a wife and two kids. Please don't turn me in."

Being a commander means facing awful choices on a regular basis. Being a Christian meant I had to find not just the right answer, but the right answer presented in Christ's way.

"I'm not going to make a decision on your future today. You won't fly for the remainder of this trip because I don't trust you right now. You may have a wife and two kids, but I have twenty men on that plane to think about. I also have their wives and children to think about if something goes wrong. When we get home, we're going to get you some help. Then we'll see what to do after that."

When we returned home, we entered him into a base rehabilitation program. It was a kind of "Scared Straight" program that took problem drinkers through a drunk tank, an emergency room, and a morgue on a Friday night.

As often happens in the military, I was transferred before seeing the conclusion of this story. However, I called back a year later to talk to a friend who had taken over as squadron commander. I asked how the captain was doing.

"You won't believe it. He really cleaned up his act."

"Not only that, he started treating his family better and was promoted to major on the last board."

I hung up the phone with a smile on my face; a surge of joy passed through my heart. It was what every commander lives for—to make a difference in the life of a service member and his family. I breathed a "thank You, Lord" and turned back to finish the pile of paperwork on my desk. Moments like these, I thought, made even the paperwork tolerable.

A WARRIOR'S PASSING

★

MAJOR ERIC KAIL
US ARMY

Nevertheless, to the degree that we have already attained,
let us walk by the same rule, let us be of the same mind.
Brethren, join in following my example, and note those who so
walk, as you have us for a pattern (Phil. 3:16-17).

It was a warm sunny morning, like all the other mornings a young boy enjoys growing up in Hawaii. My dad had just returned from his second tour in Vietnam. He had served thirty-two years in the army, rising to the rank of colonel while commanding at the company, battalion and brigade levels. The traditions, strengths, and values of the military were deeply embedded in him, and in turn, he taught them to me.

That day we were taking a family outing that would forever define my impression of my dad's character. After a short drive, we stood as a family by a chain link fence. We formed a small part of a large crowd that watched an airplane land on a military runway. I was only six, but I had seen planes land before, so I watched Dad's face for an explanation of what was special about this one.

After what seemed hours, the plane door opened and a couple of men in uniform walked down onto the runway. One of them even stopped for a moment to kiss the ground. He was one of the last returning POWs from Vietnam. Looking up to Dad, I stopped short of asking a question and instead simply stared at him.

The emotions I saw on his face defined in an instant the character I still strive to emulate: Selfless *pride* in knowing that he was brother to these men; joy in the fact that their prayers had been answered; a brief *sadness* that they had been made to persevere through suffering for so long; and *peace* in the knowledge that their homecoming was at last taking place. That day remains my earliest and most lasting memory; it was also the beginning of a very young boy making a commitment to be like his father someday.

Dad was the epitome of an American country boy from the Midwest. He was honest, reliable, and brutally straightforward. Though never obsessed with perfection, he was a man committed to high standards and craftsmanship. When I was a young cadet, he gave me a verse that clearly explained his work ethic: "If racing against mere men makes you tired, how will you race against horses? If you stumble and fall on open ground, what will you do in the thickets near the Jordan?" (Jer. 12:5 NLT). On the day I graduated from Ranger School, he gave me a big hug and said, "Run with the horses, Bud!"

My dad identified strongly with a centurion named Cornelius mentioned in the Bible; a man of duty, leadership, and faith. Dad was a true warrior; therefore, he manifested an aggressive drive for the care and development of other warriors. He believed that sitting on the sidelines was a cheap way of life, so he consistently exhorted those he knew to get into the game. One of my favorite soldierly heirlooms from him hangs in my office doorway. No one can enter without seeing the small brass-and-wood plaque that reads, "Do *something* . . . lead, follow, or get out of the way!"

Dad had many passions. He loved his family and the great outdoors. He would stop whatever he was doing to brag on his grandkids or talk about fly-fishing and elk hunting. At the top of his list, however, was bringing the Good News of Christ to our military.

We said our last good-byes to my father as we buried him on a crisp November morning at Arlington National Cemetery. I will miss him. He left a legacy of faith and stewardship worthy of a prince. In our sorrow, we should follow his example with *selfless pride* that he was a brother in arms, *joy* that his prayer has been answered, brief *sadness* that he needed to persevere through suffering in the flesh, and *peace* knowing that his homecoming has taken place.

(Used by permission of Command magazine, published by Officers' Christian Fellowship, Englewood, Colorado.)

SIR, I'M PREGNANT

★

Finally, all of you be of one mind,
have compassion for one another . . . (1 Peter 3:8).

You have turned for me my mourning into dancing; You have put
off my sackcloth and clothed me with gladness (Ps. 30:11).

While Air Force Academy cadets wear uniforms, at heart they are college kids. While they have a far different lifestyle than most college students, their antics and pranks rival many of their civilian peers. Many are enormously successful and graduate as Fulbright and Rhodes Scholars, while others are eliminated or drop out.

Becoming a cadet involves a highly competitive process ending with a recommendation from a member of Congress. The Scripture that says "Many are called, but few are chosen" certainly applies here. Unlike mainstream university students, cadets are not allowed to marry or have children. The significance of that rule struck me, as an AOC (Air Officer Commanding), when a female cadet reported to my office one day and asked for permission to come in. Then she asked if she could close the door.

Big alarm bells went off in my head at her request. As she sat down she stumbled through several unintelligible words before blurting out miserably, "Sir, I'm pregnant."

Considering how miserable she appeared, this clearly wasn't a statement of good news and joy. She understood that she couldn't continue at the Academy in her condition. I could only imagine what it cost her to come to me with this news. So I told her, "I want you to know I am very proud of you for the decision you've already made. You could have gone downtown, taken care of your pregnancy with an abortion, and no one here would have been the wiser. It's clear to me that you value the life you carry, otherwise we wouldn't be speaking now."

The tears began to pour down her face. She shook her head

affirming what I had said.

"Second, I will help you in every way I can to work through the process of your pregnancy and your future here at the Academy. Your future here is a realistic possibility should you choose it. However, you face a detour in your immediate plans."

For the first time, she looked up with hope in her eyes. As a commander, the most important thing we can do is make a positive difference in the lives of those we supervise. As a believer, my goal is to treat each subordinate as I would like to be treated. I'd made my share of mistakes, and it wasn't my place to judge the young woman who sat before me.

Over the next few weeks, I helped her through the steps of out-processing the Academy and notifying her parents, the father-to-be, and the command structure above me. The best I could do, I felt, was to walk beside her as far as I could. There were no words that could change her circumstances. I wanted her to see the love of Christ through my actions and support.

Like the woman caught in adultery, she needed no one to condemn her—she already was doing a fine job of condemning herself. What she needed was someone to help her see that this wasn't the end; there was hope ahead. The day came for her to leave and I wished her and her family well as they loaded their vehicles with all her possessions. I watched them drive away with sadness as I returned to the other 125 cadets in my squadron. A month or so passed, and I received a letter from the mother of my former cadet:

> Sir, first things first. Thank you. You made a difficult situation a lot easier for my daughter and her dad. It is a hard thing for us, but I know God will give us strength. Our daughter has come a long way, and I don't want her to feel she is a failure. I know she wants to finish her studies at the Academy, and if she is allowed to return, it will be hard, very hard. But I believe in her. I hope she makes the right decision, but it will be difficult. I'm sure you figured out her dad and I have different opinions; I want her to go to term and have

the baby. I want her to give the world a great person who can bring joy and love to us (after all the pain and sorrow).

You have been a true "officer and gentleman," and I wish you and your family all the happiness God can bestow upon you. My daughter was wrong and admits it. She has grown and learned from past mistakes and has become a better person. May God look down on her and help her now when she needs Him so.

I put down the letter and said a prayer for the family and the decisions they faced. Later that year, I learned God heard my prayers as well as those of the mother. The world saw a new child arrive and the grandparents adopted her as their own. The cadet returned to the Academy a year later and finished her education. Sometimes I think we aren't ready or willing to take the path that's shortest or straightest. Yet even on our detours from His best, God is able to bring good out of our most dismal failings.

LEADER LED REVIVAL — IN THE CONFEDERATE ARMY

★

LT. COL. KEVIN DOUGHERTY
US ARMY

When leaders lead in Israel, When the people willingly offer themselves, Bless the Lord! (Judg. 5:2).

Ever wonder how much leaders can do to encourage those beneath them toward or away from the Lord? If so, you might be surprised to learn how He has used godly leaders to bring many to Him, even in the most unlikely places. Sometimes this occurred among those considered least likely to receive Him. This is one such story.

> I have never seen such a spirit as there is now in the army. Religion is the theme. Everywhere, you hear around the campfires at night the sweet songs of Zion. This spirit pervades the whole army. God is doing glorious work. . . . If this state of things should continue for any considerable length of time, we will have in the Army of Tennessee an army of believers.[12]

Thus wrote a Confederate soldier in the spring of 1864. In the late winter and spring of 1863, and again in the winters of 1863-1864 and 1864-1865, great revivals swept the Confederate Army. The Reverend John Jones estimated that 150,000 Confederate soldiers made professions of faith during the war.[13]

In the winter of 1863-1864 alone, 15,000 soldiers of the Army of Northern Virginia were converted.[14] There were reports of 200 baptisms in a single day and often more than 2,000 soldiers attending services.[15]

What brought about such numbers? "The Christian example of

the Confederate high command; the concerted efforts of Southern churches to provide the army with tracts and preachers; the character of the Confederate soldier; the optimism that accompanied victory; and the fear that accompanied the ever-present prospect of death."[16]

It is hard to overestimate the impact that the Christian example of men like Robert E. Lee and Stonewall Jackson had on Confederate soldiers. Their prayerfulness, selflessness, reverence for God's law, humility, and attitude of service are all well chronicled. Less well known is that the Confederate high command, especially Lee and Jackson, actively pursued the great revival in the army. They saw themselves as leading an army of God, and they used their positions to create the conditions for a spiritual awakening.

"Jackson planned personally to superintend . . . a new awakening. His devotion would be the catalyst."[17] Lee also was intimately connected with the revival. His chaplains reported that as they briefed him on its progress, "we saw his eyes brighten and his whole countenance glow with pleasure."[18] Jackson's wife, Anna, wrote that, "the constant attendance of General Jackson and frequent appearance of General Lee and other distinguished officers soon drew out vast crowds of soldiers . . . leading them to follow the great Captain to their salvation."[19]

Perhaps the most famous Confederate revival occurred at Jackson's camp in the winter of 1862-1863. The seeds of this revival were planted in the preaching of Joseph Stiles and A.M. Marshall as they ministered to Jackson's army around Winchester, Virginia, in November 1862. These chaplains led a series of camp meetings that succeeded "in fanning this religious feeling into the spiritual fire of the great revival that subsequently spread through the army."[20]

After the battle of Fredericksburg, Jackson made his winter headquarters at Moss Neck to rest and reorganize. He told his chief of staff, Major Robert Dabney, to make "unusual efforts . . . for the spiritual improvement of the Army."[21] He appointed Tucket Lacy as his "chaplain-general" and formed the Second Corps Chaplains' Association. Robertson wrote, "No field commander thought chaplains more important than Jackson."[22]

Jackson's men quickly built log chapels throughout the camp, and attendance at the services was formidable.[23]

Much of the groundwork for the revival was laid by the massive distribution (often through civilian organizations) of Bibles, religious literature, and tracts. In addition to this wealth of printed materials, eminent civilian preachers flocked to the Confederate camps to preach the gospel. The connection between spiritual awakening and the high tide of pamphleteering and preaching was unmistakable.[24]

All of us have people who watch and see what sort of Christian example we set. Most of us also have some degree of leadership responsibility, which includes the spiritual well-being of those we serve with. Lee and Jackson worked to create the conditions that would lead to the eternal salvation of their men.

G.F.R. Henderson wrote, "Taught by Lee, Jackson, (Jeb) Stuart, and many others . . . the Southern soldiers . . . discovered that purity and temperance are by no means incompatible with military prowess, and that a practical piety, faithful in small things as in great, detracts in no degree from skill and resolution in the field."[25]

None of the factors that established the foundation for revival in the Confederate Army were beyond the ability of God in cooperation with the godly influence of Lee and Jackson. May we each be found faithful to the trust He gives us when we are placed in positions of responsibility and leadership.

(Used by permission of Command magazine, published by Officers' Christian Fellowship, Englewood, Colorado.)

A TIME
FOR HUMILITY

*Humility is a strange thing. The minute
you think you've got it, you've lost it.*

E.D. Hulse

*Do not consider yourself to have made any
spiritual progress, unless you account
yourself the least of all men.*

Thomas à Kempis

*Abraham Lincoln,
His hand and pen,
He will be good,
But God knows when.*

Abraham Lincoln—as a child

DESPISING THE SHAME

★

Looking unto Jesus, the author and finisher of our faith,
who for the joy that was set before Him endured the cross,
despising the shame, and has sat down at the
right hand of the throne of God (Heb. 12:2).

I never really understood the meaning of the Scripture "Jesus endured the cross, despising the shame" until I had a very bad day as a young navigator. I'd begun my career some two years earlier and had made a strong start. When I completed my training, I was sent to my first operational B-52 assignment in Sacramento, California. I hit the ground running and was working hard to find my place and establish my reputation as a young lieutenant. The Lord was about to get my attention in an unexpected way.

The B-52 was older than any of us who flew it and needed constant maintenance and upgrades to keep it in the air. My crew station (my position on the aircraft) was being completely re-configured. When I arrived, only three of the wing's seventeen planes had this new configuration. As a result, I flew the old system most of the time, and had only superficial training and knowledge of the new.

One day, during a pre-flight weather briefing, a senior captain walked up to me from the squadron and said, "I'm here to give you a no-notice check ride." Those words will strike fear in the heart of most aviators. For the next eight hours, I would be observed by a very qualified flight officer during every phase of flight. All of my actions would be recorded and later debriefed for errors. If my actions didn't meet standards, I would receive a "less than qualified" rating, which would take me off the flying schedule until I was retrained. For a flyer, that would be devastating.

I walked to the airplane, looked at the tail number, and froze. This plane was modified with the newest configuration. *Now what were the chances I'd get this jet to fly?* I thought with dismay. I went through the flight, fumbling around as I tried to familiarize myself with the knobs, dials, and switches. After the flight was over, I knew I'd blown it. I was ruled "less than qualified."

I left the debrief in shock thinking my career was over. The other officers looked at me as if I were a leper. There was personal disappointment and, yes, shame over my performance. I read the Bible for comfort and discovered the verse, "who for the joy set before him, endured the cross, despising the shame . . ."

How was it possible that Jesus could despise the shame, when I was overwhelmed with it? He was dragged from His friends, ridiculed, and railroaded by the religious leaders, brutalized by the Romans, derided by the crowds, and *still* He despised the shame. Then I saw it. He was looking *beyond the moment* to the joy of what was before Him—the salvation of His people. Suddenly, I realized that the circumstances of my failure were temporary while my *future* was secure in Him. Why should I be ashamed of that? I was both comforted and re-motivated.

About a month later the evaluator who had disqualified me said, "I'm really impressed by your attitude and your effort. Clearly, this was a problem of training, not your competence." I kept my head up, finished my re-training and was put back on qualified status again. The end of this story is equally remarkable. I discovered the evaluator was a believer and we developed a friendship that has lasted to this day. Some fifteen years after that check-ride, while he was commanding a flying squadron, he called and asked me to be his second in command—his operations officer! Now, isn't that just like the Lord?

THE LAUNDRY KING

★

His lord said to him, "Well done, good and faithful servant;
you were faithful over a few things, I will make you ruler over
many things. Enter into the joy of your lord" (Matt. 25:21).

I joined the air force and went through Officer Training School. The one thing I took with me to this school was motivation. I had a wife and two children. I'd been managing a restaurant and had no desire to return to that. Failure was not an option.

Halfway through the program I was interviewed for a leadership position in the trainee wing. Each of us who was selected would get a key position. I envisioned being selected for command of a squadron or a group or the entire wing. However, as I was later told, I was a little *too* enthusiastic. I was not chosen for a wing, group, or squadron command position. In fact, I wasn't chosen for any key staff position. Yet, because my performance in the program had been outstanding, the school's leadership wanted me to have *something*.

That something was to take control of the maintenance and supervision of the vending machines and washers and dryers that were on the school grounds. With the job I earned the unofficial nickname of the "Laundry King."

Even though the job was considered small, I wanted to be faithful and give my best. A lot of folks thought the position hilarious, while others consoled me on not getting a better job. I attacked the job with all the energy I could muster.

The machines were located in four buildings on numerous floors. I discovered that many washers, dryers, and vending machines were out of order. In fact, in one building with four floors, where a hundred trainees lived, only two washers worked. Ten were out of order.

I discovered the vending companies responsible for the machines weren't aware of the problem because there wasn't a systematic way to notify them when their machines broke down.

Consequently, I set up a system where residents would notify me of breakdowns and I would arrange for repair.

Within about two weeks, the machines that had been broken were repaired or replaced. That should have been the end of the entire affair. Problem fixed; I graduate and move on. However, I wasn't aware that this had been a long-standing problem. Suddenly, the school's leaders no longer received frequent complaints.

One day during class, my flight commander received a hand-delivered message ordering me to report to the school commandant. The distance in rank between me and that colonel was as far as the moon to the earth. It could only be bad news. I walked the quarter mile between my classroom and the commandant's head-quarters very slowly. I wracked my brain to figure out what I had done wrong. Well, I figured I'd done plenty wrong, but what was bad enough to get me called down to the commandant's office?

As I was ushered into his office, the colonel looked at me and said, "I've got two groups in this wing, one that has working washing machines and dryers and one that doesn't. Your group seems to have solved this problem, and I want to know how you did it." A direct question like that deserved a direct answer and I gave it to him. Soon all the people in the chain below him knew why I'd been called to his office.

Three weeks later, I heard my name called out as a distinguished graduate (DG) as I received my gold bars. A number of squadron commanders, a group commander, and others who had been given key staff positions weren't selected as DGs. But the guy they called the "Laundry King" was honored, I believe, for being faithful even in the smallest of things.

HOW MANY MIGS DID YOU SHOOT DOWN?

★

For not from the east or from the west and not from the wilderness comes lifting up; but it is God who executes judgment, putting down one and lifting up another (Ps. 75:6,7 RSV).

We live in a fairly self-centered "instant" culture—fast food, instant fame, overnight jackpots, and everything in between. The idea of "me-first" has long since replaced "after-you" in our cultural vocabulary. So it should have come as no surprise to see these attitudes show up among our younger troops. The military emphasizes the very biblical idea of "service before self," a concept of servanthood that conflicts with our "me first" culture. As a commander, I ran into a conflict of these two "values" and tried to emphasize what I considered the virtue over the vice.

I had been promoted on time through major and didn't consider myself a "fast-burner" (military slang for being promoted early). I'd been selected to attend the Naval War College and was excited to have the opportunity to attend a sister-service school.

My year went extraordinarily well. I graduated first in my class, and six months later I was promoted early. That was my first "below-the-zone" promotion, and suddenly I was a fast-burner without a clue!

A friend of mine was also promoted two years early on the same board. One afternoon we sat down to compare notes. For me, I'd had a very solid career that got kicked into after-burner when I graduated first in my class from the Navy School.

He told me he had flown during Desert Storm. He was an F-15 pilot who'd caught the first few days of the war flying combat air patrol in Iraq. He had spotted two MIGs crossing the thirty-third parallel and launched two air-to-air missiles at them. The first exploded on impact while the second went into a spin and exploded on the ground. In the period of thirty seconds he'd gone from "average crew dog" to air force Hero. He shook his head, chuckled, and said, "I was just doing my job."

As a commander, you get a lot of folks who come in for career counseling. Since I was now part of a very select group of the top two percent of the officer corps, I got a lot of questions that generally began, "Can you tell me how you got promoted so early?"

The young folks I was counseling had between one to ten years of experience, and were looking for a quick shortcut to stardom. I didn't see things working that way. Finally, after about the twentieth officer sauntered through my door asking how he could get promoted early, I decided enough was enough.

I had to better communicate the virtue of servanthood, not because it was the route to glory, but because it was the basis of great leadership and the foundation for true contentment. The glory they sought was both momentary and capricious—much like my friend's experience during the war. He just happened to be in the air when the war kicked off.

I called the squadron together and asked them all to stand up. I said, "Okay, now everyone here who shot down a MIG in Desert Storm remain standing. Everyone else sit down." Everyone sat down and looked confused.

"A lot of folks have been asking me how they can get promoted early. They think I've got some magic formula, or that my career is a template they can copy. I don't think so. Frankly, I think the chances of getting promoted early are only a little better than shooting down a MIG in a conflict you might be in someday. That's how a friend of mine was just recently selected for early promotion. He was in the right place at the right time on the right side of two lethal missiles.

"My advice to you is this: stop trying to figure out how to beat the system. Start figuring out how to become the best at your job you can be. Work a little smarter, work a lot harder. Then, the air force might recognize you. Then, your peers might admire you. And if neither of those things happen, you can look yourself in the mirror in the morning and be proud of what you see. Dismissed!"

THE BRIDGE ON THE RIVER KWAI . . . THE REST OF THE STORY

★

CAPTAIN ART ATHENS

USMS (U.S. MERCHANT MARINE ACADEMY)

Not by might, nor by power, but by my Spirit,
saith the Lord of hosts (Zech. 4:6b KJV).

One of my favorite movies is the Academy Award winner *The Bridge on the River Kwai*. While the movie is both spectacular and suspenseful, the real story is quite different.

Ernest Gordon provides "the rest of the story" of the Chungkai prison camp, which was seventy-five miles west of Bangkok on the banks of the River Kwai. A company commander in the Ninety-third Highlanders, Gordon spent three and one-half years as a prisoner of war. Much of this time was in Chungkai.

In his book *Through the Valley of the Kwai*, Gordon describes a camp marked by sickness, death, and despair. The thin veneer of civilization had been peeled back, exposing a community of men filled with hatred, hopelessness, and disregard for one another. "When a man lay dying we had no words of mercy. When he cried for our help, we averted our heads. Men cursed the Japanese, their neighbors, themselves, and God. Cursing became such an obsession that they constructed whole sentences in which every word was a curse." In the midst of this darkness, God did something extraordinary. It was so extraordinary that Hollywood could never portray, it and those affected would never be the same.

Stricken with amebic dysentery, malaria, and diphtheria, Gordon was dying with no more hope than the hundreds who had gone before him. The difference for Gordon, and eventually the whole camp, was two men: "Dusty" Miller and "Dinty" Moore. Two men who responded to the words of Jesus, "As the Father sent Me, I also send you" (John 20:21, NAS). Two men who obeyed Paul's exhortation to the Thessalonians, "Pray without ceasing" (1 Thess. 5:17). Two men who believed, "Greater love has no one than this, than to lay down one's life for his friends" (John 15:13). As living epistles, Miller and Moore washed Gordon's wounds, attended to his sores, shared their own meager rations, and massaged his lifeless legs, ministering as much to his spirit as to his body. They were "Jesus in the flesh" to Gordon.

As the story of this and other acts of self-sacrifice circulated around the camp, people started to treat one another with respect and love. Groups began to study the life of Jesus. Released from captivity to sin, creative minds devised anesthetics from plants and artificial limbs from bamboo shoots. The prisoners established a university, a forty-piece orchestra, and a church without walls. Real life returned to Chungkai.

Gordon stated, "Ours was a church of the spirit. It was the throbbing heart which gave life to the camp and transformed it in considerable measure from a mass of frightened individuals into a community. From it we received the inspiration that made life possible. Such inspiration was not merely a rosy glow in the abdomen, but the literal in-breathing of the Holy Spirit that enabled men to live nobler lives, to become kind neighbors, to create improvements for the good of others, including such mundane matters as learning to cook better rice. God's kind and creative Spirit was clearly in evidence."

Chungkai became saturated with God, awakened and transformed, as He had come in power. As radio commentator Paul Harvey would say, "And now you know . . . the rest of the story."

But the story doesn't really end there. At least it shouldn't. What occurred in Chungai over fifty years ago can occur today at Fort Hood, Langley Air Force Base, Camp Pendleton, and Norfolk Naval Base. It can occur aboard ships at sea and in the classrooms at academies and ROTC units. The challenge and opportunity before each of us is to become, like Miller and Moore, living epistles to those around us.

(Used by permission of Command magazine, published by Officers' Christian Fellowship, Englewood, Colorado.)

A Time
To Serve

The best servant does his work unseen.
Oliver Wendell Holmes

He rises by lifting others.
Robert G Ingersoll

There is no greater satisfaction for a just and well-meaning person than the knowledge that he devoted his best energies to the service of the good cause.
Albert Einstein

A KINGDOM RULED BY FEAR

★

There is no fear in love; but perfect love casts out fear . . .
(1 John 4:18).

Scripture tells us that God did not give us a spirit of fear. That spirit comes from the enemy of our souls, who rules his kingdom with an enslaving power that brings fear to those under his rule. I never understood the incredible difference between the two until I was on military business in the Mediterranean. I had been serving as a UN peacekeeper in the Middle East just prior to the Gulf War. Part of my ordinary duties was to cross between various countries that barely co-existed.

To enter one particular Middle Eastern country,[26] I had to cross two series of checkpoints. Much like crossing the old Checkpoint Charlie in Berlin, it was a very tense hour. A lot of questions were asked of me and my driver. My vehicle was searched, and all of my bags were pulled out for examination. Every item I had in my suitcases was carefully examined—every item. If they found something they considered improper they could seize it, seize me, or refuse me entry into their country. Because I had been warned in advance, I carefully packed my case to avoid controversial items and ensure safe passage.

Once past this initial screening, I was on my way, though not alone. After traveling several kilometers and turning several times, I noticed we were being followed—standard procedure. Entering the downtown area of the largest city, I saw a large gray building set on top of a hill. My driver said it was a prison. I noticed it lacked a fence and asked why.

"Oh," my driver said matter-of-factly, "when you go to prison in this country you go to prison. If your sentence is fifteen years, that's how long you spend in your cell. You don't come out for meals or exercise or anything else."

I was still trying to comprehend his statement when we entered the main square. I was shocked to see two corpses hanging there. My driver explained, "This reminds the population of the penalties for failing to follow the law." As we neared the apartment building where I would stay, I noticed a number of guards on the buildings carrying automatic weapons. The driver informed me that there were more than a dozen secret police organizations in the country to keep order. When my driver said his good-byes, he added, "Be careful what you say and do in here. I expect the whole place is bugged."

That highlighted for me in a way I never understood before the difference between God's kingdom and Satan's. God rules with love. His love is infinite and everlasting. He desires to wrap us in His safe and loving arms, well away from the kingdom of fear and the enemy who rules there. Satan is a liar, a deceiver who only destroys, bringing pain and every evil thing.

While my experience was a wake-up call to the differences between the two, it pales in comparison with the true kingdom of fear. When I cross paths with people enslaved to fear and anger, I try to remember that their behavior reflects the ruler of that kingdom, and I pray for the opportunity to share with them about the kingdom I live in. My King's law is love, enforced with love and demonstrated in the sacrificial life of Jesus Christ. I can't think of another place I'd rather live.

SOUTHERN BELLES ARE NOT SOLDIERS!

★

LT .COL. PENNY BAILEY
USAF

If you want to be my follower you must love me more than your own father and mother, wife and children, brothers and sisters—yes, more than your own life. Otherwise, you cannot be my disciple
(Luke 14:26 NLT).

I grew up in a traditional family, raised to become a "lady." Now when I say traditional, I mean southern traditional—southern belles, debutante balls, wedding bells, baby bells, in that order. But at age ten, I felt a call from God that put me at odds with the life my family envisioned for me.

In a Sunday school class the teacher asked each of us, "What do you want to be when you grow up?"

Everyone seemed to have an answer, but I had never given it much thought. I was having too much fun being a kid to think of such things. Anyway, when she got to me I answered honestly and said, "I don't know."

She looked at me and said, "Well, you need to think about it," and went on to the next child. After church, I went home thinking hard about what I should be when I grew up. Finally, it came to me.

I ran into the kitchen and told Mom, "I know what I'm going to be when I grow up."

"Oh really, what's that?" she replied.

"A nun!" I said and beamed.

She smiled and patted me on the head and said "Sweetheart, Southern Baptists can't be nuns."

After she explained the whole thing to me, I was very disappointed. So I went back and began to pray about it. "God, what is it that I can do to serve You and serve my country?"

It was the height of the Cold War, and I was very aware that children in China and Russia weren't allowed to worship God. I also wanted to do something to thank America for allowing me the freedom to worship God.

As I prayed, an answer formed in my mind that was clear and strong. I was thrilled by the thought and ran to tell my mom.

"Mom, this time I *know* what I'm going to be."

"What's that?"

"I'm going to be a soldier."

She smiled and patted me on the head again and explained that girls couldn't be in the military.

This time I wasn't discouraged. I just knew that this was what I would do someday.

As I neared completion of college, I was contacted by a recruiter who encouraged me to quit college, join the army, and finish my degree at night. When I mentioned this to my parents, they went ballistic. I quickly changed the subject and decided to put off any further discussions until after college.

One day my sorority sister asked me to go with her to see the air force recruiter. I told her, "No way. My parents would kill me. They'd never let me join."

"You don't understand," she said, "*I* want to talk to the recruiter. I just want you to come along and hold my hand."

Well, that seemed pretty non-threatening, so I went along. By the time the recruiter finished she had decided no, but I decided—go!

But now I was faced with the task of informing my parents. I decided to talk with my dad first and asked if we could have dinner together. We had a nice dinner, and afterward, he looked at me and said, "Okay, now what's this all about? I know there's something up, and I want to know what it is."

"Well, Dad," I began slowly, "I joined the air force but I get to stay in school. I'll make some money every month, and I'll have a good job when I get out."

He thought it over and decided that was okay with him. Then he dropped the bomb. "You'll have to come home this weekend and tell your mom."

"But Dad, that's why I called you here. You can tell Mom."

"No way," he said firmly. "You're going to tell her, but I'll be there with you."

That Friday night I drove home but Dad wasn't there. He had to work late. I kept looking out the window for him, but before he showed up, Mom said, "So what's up? Your dad says you have something to tell me."

I swallowed hard and blurted out, "I joined the air force. But I get to stay in school. I'll make some money every month, and I'll have a good job when I get out."

Her face went blank. She didn't say a word. She turned away from me, picked up the phone, and began to dial. When someone answered, Mom said, "Hello, Mom. Penny has something to tell you."

This was my maternal grandmother. If you know anything about a southern family, you know that if you're in with Grandmother, you're in with the family. If you're out with Grandmother, you're out with everyone else.

I said, "Grandmother, it's the greatest thing. You're going to be so happy for me. I'm going to be an officer in the air force. I get to stay in school, make $100 a month, and I'll have a great job when I get out!"

Silence was followed by more silence. Then, very sternly, she said, "You know what kind of girls join the military?"

I was in total shock. "But Grandmother, this is me. I've been a Christian all my life. You know I'm going to be a good girl."

"Let me speak to your mother," she said firmly.

Mom took the phone and all she said was "Yes, ma'am. Yes, ma'am" and then hung up. With tears in her eyes she walked into her bedroom and closed the door. I saw my life as a southern belle close as well. We never did have dinner that night.

I left the next morning with a heavy heart as my prayers for reconciliation went up to heaven. I wondered how other members of my family would treat me and whether they would ever accept my choice. I guess that was the day I really grew up.

As the months passed, my family slowly warmed up to me

again. I was grateful for that. But most of all, I was grateful that God had strengthened me when I faced the choice of following Him or the seemingly safe life of a southern belle. I've had eighteen incredible years of serving the Lord and serving my country. Being a Christian in the military has been a great challenge and a great opportunity. I could have missed it, except I learned that God's quiet leading is more powerful than the strongest opposition.

HOMEWARD BOUND

★

LT. CLEMENT KETCHUM
US NAVAL RESERVE

Foxes have holes and birds of the air have nests, but the Son of Man has nowhere to lay his head (Matt. 8:20).

As members of the military, we know what it is like to move every few years, and to live a life that is generally on the move. I have often heard people say, "It will be nice to settle down." But will it? Does God have words to say on this subject?

In 1996, I left the Coast Guard. My family and I had decided to go into ministry with Mercy Ships, the sea-going arm of Youth With a Mission. While I was preparing to leave active duty, my supervisor in the Coast Guard wanted to talk. He genuinely liked me and cared about what would happen to me. Mercy Ships is a volunteer organization, and I would be required to raise my support. "What about tuition for your children's college? What about retirement?" He asked all the usual questions.

In reality he wasn't asking so much as he was saying, "You won't have money for your kids' college tuition; you won't have a way to retire and settle down." It was almost as if he were writing the final chapter of my life! I answered by telling him the Lord had been faithful to me. I had been around the world and had done some wonderful things. In short, the "Book of Clem" wasn't finished yet. And I can say that so far I like the story. It will be interesting to see how God will write my final chapter.

Since that conversation, I have been reminded again and again that life in the Lord is dynamic and ever changing. Yet, many Christians set stability and retirement as their goals. What they do not realize is that arriving at a goal, realizing stability, or achieving retirement are all just chapters in the book. They are just ports on the voyage, not the final chapter or destination.

I'm not advocating recklessness nor arguing against personal financial planning or family security. I am saying that these should not be our primary focus. Jesus never encouraged His disciples to develop retirement plans. When one said, "Lord, first let me go and bury my father," Jesus responded, "Follow Me, and let the dead bury their own dead." In fact, He probably surprised His disciples when he informed them that He himself was seeing to their retirement. And it wouldn't come while living in these mortal bodies. He said, "In my Father's house are many rooms; if it were not so, I would have told you. I am going there to prepare a place for you" (John 14:2 NIV).

The next time the orders come to move or deploy, consider our Lord Jesus Christ, Paul, and the other apostles who also lived life "on the move." Be encouraged as you transition (again and again), as you deploy and find yourself on a new assignment, or even in a new career. As you take steps toward where God is leading you, remember each day is another day on the voyage home.

(Used by permission of Command magazine, published by Officers' Christian Fellowship, Englewood, Colorado.)

"*As a man of war that sails through the sea, so this earth sails through the air. We mortals are all on board a fast-sailing, never sinking world-frigate, of which God was the shipwright; and she is but one craft in a Milky-Way fleet, of which God is the Lord High Admiral. The port we sail from is ever astern. And though far out of sight of land, for ages and ages we continue to sail with sealed orders, and our last destination remains a secret to ourselves and our officers; yet our final haven was predestined ere we slipped from the stocks of Creation. . . .*

Believe not the hypochondriac dwellers below hatches, who will tell you, with a sneer, that our world-frigate is bound to no final harbor whatever; that our voyage will prove an endless circumnavigation of space. . . .

Whatever befall us, let us never train our murderous guns inboard; let us not mutiny with bloody pikes in our hands. Our Lord High Admiral will yet interpose; and though long ages should elapse, and leave our wrongs un-redressed, yet, shipmates and world-mates let us never forget that,

"Whoever afflict us, whatever surround,

Life is a voyage that's homeward bound!"

Herman Melville, White Jacket

A Time
To Lose

They who lose today may win tomorrow.
Cervantes, Don Quixote

He loseth nothing who keeps God for his friend.
John Ray

Good God, man, history is full of examples of battles being lost because units stopped on the near side of a river.
George Patton

It's not what they take away from you that counts. It's what you do with what you have left. Never give up and never give in.
Hubert Humphrey

MILITARY LIFE AND REAL ESTATE DON'T MIX

★

*Deliver me in Your righteousness, and cause me to
escape; Incline Your ear to me, and save me. Be my
strong habitation, To which I may resort continually;
You have given the commandment to save me,
For You are my rock and my fortress* (Ps. 71:2-3).

If the trick to real estate was "buy high and sell low," my wife and I
would be on every TV talk show because we've mastered the concept. You'd have to call us optimists, because with each move, we'd
fall in love with the new location and think "this is it!" Two to three
years later we were on the move again. After eighteen moves in
twenty-five years of marriage, we've learned that owning real estate
and being in the military generally aren't compatible.

When we arrived in Alaska at the peak of the oil boom in the late
1980s, housing was in extremely short supply. What was available
was expensive. The base housing list was a mile long, so my wife and
I did our best to locate relatively reasonable housing in the area. We
were blessed to find a couple selling their house for $10,000 below
the appraised price. We liked the house and we bought it.

The time in Alaska went quickly and three years later, we
received orders to move. The sad thing was that housing had
dropped along with the price of oil. Our house now appraised for
$28,000 less than what we bought it for. We decided to rent it out.

The rent covered the payments until our renter, eighteen months
later, received orders to move in the middle of winter. Then our faith
was to be severely tested. At our Bible study, I shared about the need
to sell or rent our house. Our group began to pray with us on a regular basis. In my heart, I knew the Lord understood the situation.

However, the day came for the renters to move out, and no one
was ready to move in. The monthly mortgage payment was $1,400,
a lot more than we could afford. We scraped together the first

month's mortgage payment, and continued to fervently pray for God's deliverance.

We resisted turning the house back to the bank, but clearly we were on our way to defaulting on our mortgage. A reappraisal shocked us—the house now was worth $38,000 less than what we owed on it. We couldn't afford to sell it and couldn't find anyone to rent it.

One afternoon, I received a call from a realtor in Alaska. He wondered if we had taken out private mortgage insurance. I told him we had. Then he informed me, "Most houses in this area have become un-sellable because of their drop in market value. The courts recently ruled that owners with PMI and FHA loans are entitled to sell the property at appraised value and have the loss covered by PMI. Further, I have a buyer interested in your property." I could have been knocked over with a breath. I thought this might be a scam but told the agent to send the paperwork. I had nothing to lose but the house.

Three months later our house closed and the PMI covered the deficit between what we sold the house for and what we owed. God had provided a miracle just in the nick of time.

GULF WAR SYNDROME —
I JUST KEEP PRAYING

★

PATRICIA S. TAYLOR
NAVY WIFE

Let us then approach the throne of grace with confidence,
so that we may receive mercy and find grace to help us
in our time of need (Heb. 4:16 NIV).

I guess when people look at our family they see red, white, and blue. That's probably not surprising since my husband and two of our sons served in the navy.

My husband joined the navy as a Naval Reserve Seabee in 1982. This seemed like the perfect solution to a difficult financial situation brought on by our eldest son's medical bills.

When Desert Storm broke out in 1990, my husband was sent to Saudi Arabia to serve with the 24th Detachment of the Seabees. Our son Steve was involved in the war as well, serving in the navy aboard the USS *John F. Kennedy*. About this time, I was laid off from my job. Due to the stress of our eldest son's death and two loved ones at war, I developed an ulcer and was hospitalized. It seemed like my world was spinning out of control.

I began to recover and our youngest son, Terry, became the man of the house. He was eighteen years old and worked nights at a grocery store. I spent many nights alone during the next five months. But I wasn't really alone, because I drew near to the Lord in prayer. I prayed for my husband and sons and began to depend on the Lord for my every need in a way I hadn't done before.

Many who knew us prayed for us as well. We would need every one of these life-sustaining prayers.

The war ended and my husband, A.L., returned to me in May. By August Steve came home as well, and we celebrated together.

A.L. seemed a little fatigued and confused following his return, but he returned to his job handling hot steel. I was called back to work and things seemed to finally be returning to normal.

But soon, we noticed that A.L. seemed to be having memory problems, increasing fatigue, rashes, and problems with his stomach and lungs. He also ran a low grade fever, had night sweats, and many other strange symptoms.

He went to the VA and tests turned up nothing. In 1994, his lymph nodes became very swollen. He had large hives all over. He also started running a high fever and vomiting. They admitted him to the hospital for dehydration and unknown causes. The tests were all negative, and a lymph node biopsy did not show cancer. His only diagnosis was reactive lymph nodes. After ten days of around-the-clock antibiotics, he was sent home. Slowly he got better and went back to work.

For five years he suffered a milder case of these symptoms; then they hit him again full-force. He went back into the hospital for thirteen days and another biopsy came back negative. It was very frustrating, but I learned to keep praying, to keep drawing close to the Lord and find His strength to carry me through.

A.L. retired early from his job of thirty-two years. He was just too fatigued and ill to deal with molten steel anymore. He applied for disability through the VA with high hopes, but was turned down four times. Our fifth application is now pending. Meanwhile, I just keep praying.

We believe he was exposed to nerve gas and other contaminants while in Saudi Arabia. He pushes himself to carry on, but subtle brain and nervous system damage limits his daily activity.

I've learned a lot in the past decade. In spite of everything, I still believe God is bigger than my problems. I still want my loved ones to have good health and enjoy their lives. Until that day, I will keep on believing. Until that day, I will keep on praying.

My $1,000 Learning Experience

★

Behold, I send you out as sheep in the midst of wolves.
Therefore be wise as serpents and harmless as doves (Matt. 10:16).

Life is comprised of a series of learning experiences. The price of wisdom is high, and often there's no way to gain wisdom without making our share of costly mistakes. As a young captain, I made a doozy of a mistake.

Through a Bible study group, my wife and I had become close to a family with young children. They seemed to be in difficult financial circumstances, and one night I received a call from the wife who was in tears.

She said she couldn't feed her family of four because there was no money to purchase food that week. I went to their house to see what I could do. She opened the cupboards and showed me: they were bare.

Now, I was a captain with a reasonably good income, but we also had children. It should have dawned on me that her husband, a major, should have been able to manage his finances better. But, it didn't. Still, as a Christian, I couldn't turn away. I asked what had led to these problems, and she listed a litany of bills that had eaten away at their income, including cars that needed repairs.

My heart was moved by the plight of this woman and her two small children. I wrote them a check for $1,000, and when I told my wife, she supported me. I saw a need and tried to meet it. I felt good rather than foolish. Feeling foolish came two weeks later.

A couple of Sundays after I visited them, I saw them pull into the church parking lot driving a brand new Toyota. Apparently, my gift had been used as a down payment.

My wife and I looked at each other and shook our heads. We sat in our car feeling very foolish. Reviewing our actions, we decided we would never again give money in such a way. Giving bags of groceries to those in need of food would be wiser. We didn't regret the heart God had given us toward those in need. We wouldn't change that for anything. God taught us to be wiser, but not less compassionate. It was a lesson we needed to learn.

A Time for Heroes
(Part 3)

★

CUT OFF, SURROUNDED, OUTGUNNED:
ESCAPE FROM HUE CITY, 1968

MAJOR CHUCK COFTY (RETIRED)
USMC

And the Lord shall guide thee continually, and satisfy
thy soul in drought, and make fat thy bones: and thou shalt be
like a watered garden, and like a spring of water, whose
waters fail not (Isa. 58:11, KJV).

Do you want to know how great God's grace is? When I didn't even know God, when I didn't even want God, when I thought I didn't need God, He was still watching over me. God has a way of bringing us to the point where even the strongest man runs out of strength and even the smartest man runs out of answers. It is at that moment we must decide whether we will take the hand of the only one who can save us. I came to such a point during a period of six days in 1968. Though I wouldn't turn to God for another year, this was the turning point for me. It was the moment when I realized being a tough marine wasn't going to be enough to escape my desperate circumstances. I was cut off, surrounded, outgunned, and faced almost certain death or, at best, life as a POW.

I arrived in Hue City (pronounced *weigh*) on January 28, 1968 to work with Controlled American Sources (CAS), as the Central Intelligence Agency was then known. The two CAS reps I met first were Dave Hayes and Gene Weaver (CIA cover names). Hayes was an was extremely bright, articulate, and energetic college graduate, reserve Army Ranger captain, and company man with the agency.

Weaver had served many years on the Soviet desk in Virginia and now led this operation in Hue City. He was subsequently captured and spent five and one-half years as a POW in North Vietnam.

I went to the headquarters of the First ARVN Division (Army of the Republic of Vietnam) and received a briefing on extensive troop movements and deployments. I think the American ARVN Advisor was privy to some SI (sensitive intelligence) traffic and hinted there were big things going on. We also received a CAS briefing on what they knew and felt was about to take place. I remember being issued a new Browning 9mm and several other items I would need while on this Special Branch assignment. I was never comfortable with the 9mm so I kept my .45 as well as my M-16.

On the evening of the twenty-eighth, I was sent to stay with Hayes and Weaver and their six Nung (Chinese ethnic South Vietnamese) guards at the main CAS safe house. On the morning of the twenty-ninth, I met with CAS, CRD (Army Counterintelligence), and several other agencies working within the city. All involved had extensive experience in an assortment of varied and sundry spook endeavors and operations.

I distinctly remember CAS briefing something big was in the air and it was time to develop evacuation plans. I thought that if they hadn't done this already, we were in deep kimchee. After much discussion it was decided that if we were attacked, everyone would make their way to the safe house with Weaver and Hayes. From there, we would go to the roof and signal an Air America chopper using a five-star cluster (flare).

I was not really included in the conversation. I was just a "Jarhead CI" officer. What did I know about "high level" evacuation plans? I asked, "If the whistle blows and we have to evacuate Hue, won't there be gunfire, flares, clusters, mortars, hand poppers, and the like?"

"Yes," came the reply.

"Well then," I asked, "how will the chopper figure out which is which at night?"

Needless to say, that plan never came off. We were instructed to prepare for the worst. Back at the safe house we began the arduous task of burning source reports in an old fifty-five-gallon drum.

The safe house was adjacent to the Phu Com canal that emptied into the Perfume River. The dwelling was surrounded on three sides by a hedge and fence along with a smaller fence that fronted the canal. The house overlooking it was a large two-story French dwelling, with an extensive space between the roof and second story, referred to as a false roof, which protected the residents from the oppressive heat. Much of the canal was clogged with sampan traffic that afternoon.

I walked around the house to determine entrance and exit routes and noticed a large hole in the hedge on the west side as well as a hole in the fence large enough for a man to go through. In retrospect, this discovery was the absolute providence of God.

I had lived in the bush with the grunts for so long that my deuce gear (a marine's field combat gear) was still together with approximately ten to fourteen magazines of 5.56mm ammunition and two canteens. Since I had been told our near-term operations would be nearby, I removed my canteens from the rest of my gear. Leaving those canteens behind was a big mistake that nearly cost me my life. Like most marines, I had a K-Bar (combat knife) taped to the load bearing strap, a first aid packet, four fragmentary grenades, and magazine pouches. I had always carried a Gerber Mark Two fighting knife on my cartridge belt but somehow, along with the canteens, it had become detached—dumb and dumber.

I went to bed that night thinking things were going to be all right. Sleeping in a bed, rather than on the floor or cot in a hootch, was way beyond "fine." This was a far cry from life in the bush in Ashau Valley. This was simply fine on top of fine. Now I knew why all those before me had enjoyed themselves so much in Hue.

I put the 9mm under my pillow, closed my eyes, and gave a contented sigh. I was well prepared and well protected. Nungs guarded the front as well as the rear and would fight to the death—they hated the NVA and couldn't be bought off.

THE STORM

About three o'clock in the morning, heavy automatic weapons fire coming from the west woke me. By the time I got downstairs, Hayes was already monitoring the radio.

"Both the Nung compound and Special Branch are under fire," he told me.

Though we didn't know it, all of Hue City was being enveloped by a massive attack from the DMZ to Saigon. This was supposed to be the beginning of the Tet holiday celebration.

Some celebration, I thought.

The volume of fire seemed to increase as flares, mortars, RPGs (rocket propelled grenades), Claymores (mines), frags (grenades), and artillery could now be seen and heard in the darkness.

I went out front and knelt down with the Nung facing the canal. We could barely see through the mist rising from the water. It partially obscured the houses on the other side of the canal where the weapons fire continued to grow. The streetlights in Hue were left over from the French era and gave off a dim, orangish light. No light at all would have improved the visibility. Just to the right of us I could see a "hardened bridge bunker" that led over the canal. The French had built it originally to guard access from both directions. There was an M-48 tank alongside the bunker and I could hear screams in the distance. The NVA with large packs on their backs entered house after house. Each time they went in, screaming, crying, and pleading were followed by automatic weapons fire, then silence.

These houses contained the city's elite and had been specially selected by the NVA. These doctors, lawyers, and high-ranking government personnel were systemically slaughtered. The NVA intelligence apparatus was both effective and ruthless; few survived the early morning massacre. Those not killed in this first attack were later rounded up and buried alive en-masse. Between two and three thousand bodies were later discovered in shallow graves.

I moved outside our own wire and proceeded to the intersection where the bunker and tank were. The sentries, as well as the tank crew, had been killed by advance sappers who had entered the city ahead of the main column. In the dim light I saw a column of men dressed in short pants carrying heavy loads in wicker baskets. Behind these load bearers were units of North Vietnamese regulars.

I ran back into the house and yelled at Hayes and Weaver, "We've got to get moving—NOW!" We ran out of the house and escaped through the hedge and fence hole I had found the day before.

Weaver, Hayes, six Nung, and I moved away from the advancing force through back yards, alleyways, and houses south of the canal. Before entering the street itself we stopped at a driveway gate and cautiously looked left and right. Sixty-five yards down the street in the intersection was a large contingent of NVA. This made crossing the street extremely dangerous, if not impossible. My mind raced for a solution.

Surely there were deployed flanks from this unit combing the area for resistance, I thought.

We were caught in a catch-22. We couldn't go back the way we had come and we couldn't proceed. Just to our left along the river was a single-story dwelling with one or two small outhouses in the rear.

We entered the house and found a couple and their son in obvious shock, wondering what to do. We fit right in.

We sent the couple outside and warned them to keep silent because their son was going to stay inside with us. If a firefight broke out, the NVA wouldn't care who they killed. We were pretty sure, under the circumstances, the couple wouldn't give us away.

By this time, two elite divisions of NVA had overrun the city. Though we didn't know it, we were completely cut off from escape and from help. We did know our situation was grim. We arranged a loose firing order in case we had to fight our way out. In our hearts I think we knew it was inevitable, and that we had most likely reached the end of the line. I looked around the house and thought, *this is where it ends.*

We found an opening into the attic—a good place to hide. The NVA would certainly search all the houses for people as well as food. To get into the attic we pushed a large wardrobe beneath the opening and put a chair on top of it. I climbed up on the precarious perch and then into the attic.

I had the twelve-year-old boy hand our weapons up to me, and I began to store them for safe keeping. I had nearly finished storing the weapons when we were surprised by the arrival of several hundred troops, assembling right in front of our house. They couldn't have been more than forty yards away!

We watched as the NVA dropped their packs and scattered out among the trees. They were taking a break and it gave us a little time. I began to grab the weapons again. We were up to our necks in "Charlies" and it was probably only a matter of minutes before one of them came into the house. The fact that they were relaxing was an ominous sign. It meant they controlled the city.

We quietly discussed our options, which didn't take long. With the Perfume River to the north, a large force to the west, and an even larger force moving in from the south, we were trapped. That left us three options: fight to the death, be taken prisoner, or (least likely) be rescued. I pulled the last weapon from the attic when Weaver walked into the room

"Chuck, they're coming into the house," he said quietly.

I looked across the room and saw my M-16 leaning against the wall. I pulled my .45 from my shoulder holster, cocked the hammer, and promptly fell off the chair to the floor below. The noise was deafening.

Of all the times to do something so stupid! I screamed to myself.

I jumped up with my .45 at the ready and froze. I listened and waited. Nothing seemed to be happening. I put the safety on the .45, picked up my M-16, and eased over to the louvered windows.

Passing within arm's reach at that moment were three men dressed in North Vietnamese uniforms. They weren't speaking Vietnamese. We had heard them earlier when they were slaughtering people in the houses that morning. I couldn't understand what they were saying and turned to one of the Nung.

He whispered, "No, not North Vietnamese, same me." I didn't understand so I asked him again.

"No, not North Vietnamese, same me," he repeated. Chinese! They were Chinese dressed in North Vietnamese uniforms.

As they passed by the window another Chinese came into view. He stopped in front of the window and spoke to the other three as well as a man just out of view. The one in front of me was a large-framed man, short but muscular, with a square-shaped face and a large nose. I gripped my weapon—he was so close I could smell him.

He was older and, in all probability, was the patrol leader. He spoke softly to the others as though he was giving them directions. I think that at this moment he sensed something was wrong. His body seemed to freeze as he turned his head slowly from side to side. He spoke to the boy's mother, calling her "mother" in Vietnamese. Again, he nervously turned from side to side.

I couldn't see the fifth man nor the three who had already passed by, but they were close, very close. The leader was so close I considered cutting his throat. I looked over at Hayes and ran my finger across my throat, indicating my plan. The Nungs saw me and spread out ready for action. I gently motioned toward my throat again and Hayes shook his head. He didn't want me to start yet. At that moment, the guy standing in front of me turned, walked to the door, and kicked it in. Hayes raised his Winchester Pump Shotgun Model 12 loaded with brass case double-ought buck, and pulled the trigger.

The guy took the full blast and flew backward as if he had been jerked on a rope. Amazingly, he tried to get up. I stepped into the doorway and saw the three men on the right getting up. I opened up with my M-16 on semi-automatic and killed them.

I then turned back inside and opened up on the Chinese whom Dave Hayes had originally dusted. Unfortunately, the fifth man had escaped to warn his comrades. We could hear him yelling loudly. Hayes took a position near the door and I moved toward the left front of the house and opened a hexagonal-shaped window. As it swung open, I pushed my weapon through and pulled the trigger. Several more NVA fell to the ground.

By now, the weight of their numbers started to work against us. We had surprised them, but that advantage had passed. They set up two, maybe three RPDs (light machine guns) and began raking us with small arms fire. I had killed three more when an RPG round came through the front of the house and just to my right. A large chunk of shrapnel hit the left side of my chest and knocked me to the ground. I had an M-16 magazine in the left pocket of my plated flak jacket. I reached for my pocket and both it and the magazine were gone. Putting that mag in my pocket probably saved my life as it took the brunt of the RPG shrapnel. I felt inside the flak vest to check for damage and found none. I had just had the breath knocked out of me, and I quickly got off the deck.

I pushed my weapon back through the window and managed to kill several more advancing NVA. By now, the dead and wounded were piling up in the courtyard. This was no cause for rejoicing—we knew our time was running out. Our ammo was also running out. It was just a matter of time before heavy weapons were brought to bear against us. Unless we got relief or escaped we were finished.

I noticed a tall NVA lieutenant looking over the wall. Apparently these were his men and one of the wounded in front of the house was screaming. He was trying to figure a way to get to him. I waited as he moved from the wall to the courtyard and then to the protection of a large tree. He stepped from behind the tree and ran to the man who had fallen over the others. It was there that I killed him. Of all those I killed that morning, this man often came to my mind. I wondered if he, like me, was married and had children. He was a sharp looking officer and I regretted his death. I can't say why, but God showed me my own vulnerability in his death. I would have time to reflect on this in the coming days. For now, though, we were nearly out of options.

Another RPG came through the window and the house exploded inside again.

"Dave!" I yelled. "I can't hold this position anymore. We've got to MOVE!"

We had fire coming in from three sides, but for some reason the NVA hadn't moved to seal off the rear. Dave Hayes pulled the pin on a frag and held it ready as we ran through the back door. We yelled at Weaver to come with us but he either couldn't or didn't.

"Let's go!" I yelled and ran.

We managed to clear the area behind the house without resistance. I was surprised and looked around. Dave and I were alone. We had taken off expecting everyone to follow, however, no one else came. We had been at nearly a full run for almost five minutes when Hayes called to me.

"Chuck, I've got to do something with this frag."

He held up the un-pinned frag to show me. He had his thumb on the small spoon of the frag, holding it with a death grip. We stopped and I searched the ground for something to safety it. I found a small piece of wire, ran it through the hole where the pin used to be, and crimped it tightly. As I looked at Dave and smiled at our success, I realized that he was hurt.

He had a large piece of shrapnel embedded in his leg. The round, one-inch piece of metal had penetrated his leg and rested against his femur. I helped him into what appeared to be a vacant house. It had a large hole in the ceiling, and we worked our way up through that hole into the attic area above the house.

THE EYE OF THE STORM

Resting in the attic, we tried to regain our strength before moving on. Unfortunately, our quick intelligence estimate of the vacant house had been completely, 100-percent wrong. Within a few hours we were shocked to find the NVA were using it to store their ammo. US helicopters would fly over and the NVA would open up, trying to bring them down. When their ammunition was exhausted, they would run back into the house to reload. We evaluated our situation and it wasn't good. With Dave's condition, we were going to be there for a while.

We had no food, but more importantly, we had no water. *Of all the stupid things I've done, leaving that canteen was the dumbest!* I chastised myself.

That night, the NVA came into the house to sleep. We couldn't move for fear of alerting the enemy to our presence. Talk about sleeping with the enemy!

The next day more of the same activity occurred below us. I began to wonder when these guys would leave, or when the US troops would push them out. Both Dave and I were very thirsty, but there was no relief. Another day came and went and still we couldn't move. We couldn't even move to relieve ourselves but had to urinate right where we lay. Without water, though, this wasn't a problem we had to face very often.

I had a lot of time for reflection. I wondered what happened to the Nungs and Weaver. (I later learned that ten minutes after we escaped, the house was overrun. Weaver was taken prisoner and the Nungs were all killed.)

I also began to reflect on my own life. The Lord began to catch my attention during this time. I realized that I had been preserved from some very dire circumstances. I had been very fortunate to walk out of the firefight and this wasn't the first time.

I thought about my wife, how much she loved me, and how much she wanted me to turn to the Lord. Through her, I knew many prayers were going up for me. I wondered about the effect of those prayers. I reflected on the numerous bullets that had passed me by, ambushes that had been prematurely opened, mines that were found or prematurely detonated. All pointed at something, maybe something divine, that had been protecting me.

The events of the past six months replayed for me with agonizing slowness. The more I remembered, the more difficult it was to deny something had been protecting me. Then I remembered another very close call. I hadn't previously attributed my escape from that event to anything but my skills and good luck. Lying there now, I wondered. I wondered, I reflected ,and remembered. . . .

It was June '67 and I hadn't been in country very long. I was assigned as a sub-team commander with the First Counterintelligence Team in the Phu Loc District. Late one evening, I was monitoring the radio as one of the marine patrols moved through the Cow Hai area of the district.

Hospital Corpsman (Doc) Burford was in the middle of that eighteen-man patrol consisting of both marines and some

Vietnamese Popular Forces troops know as "Pappa Foxtrots." Pappa Foxtrots were similar to our National Guard, only less trained and profoundly less organized. They normally patrolled with the marines CAPs; their strength was that they knew the terrain trails like the back of their hand.

It was nearly midnight when the peaceful night air was split with the sound of RPGs, heavy automatic weapons fire, and a sky filled with green and red tracers. Since Charlie used green tracers and we used red, there was little doubt that contact with the enemy had been made. The firefight appeared to be about three clicks (kilometers) northwest of our position and the radio cracked with conversation. We were trying to determine how bad the situation was.

The patrol leader indicated they heard the firefight but that they were not in contact with Charlie.

Not in contact with the enemy? How could that be?

A quick check of their patrol members confirmed everyone's worst fear—the patrol had split. Doc Burford, and those behind him, had taken a right fork of the trail while the main body had taken the left. This made Doc point man of a divided patrol—a deadly situation. Doc's half of the patrol was made up of several marines and five Pappa Foxtrots.

Doc had seen some movement just in front of him and then heard a noise like a "cluck." Little did he know he had just made contact with 150 NVA.

The NVA would often audibly cluck with their tongues in odd or even sequences to identify each other. The most chilling sound you could hear at night was a "cluck" nearby—you knew you had just stepped into it.

Charlie had seen them and was now attempting to identify them. When Doc did not return the "cluck" they opened fire, hitting him in both legs. Lance Corporal Laraway was carrying the M-60 and attempted to lay down a base of fire while getting Doc out of the way. In doing so, he literally threw the Doc under an overhanging scrub of low bamboo, saving the Doc's life. The VC killed Laraway just moments later along with several of the Pappa Foxtrots. Their posi tion was overrun and most of the patrol were killed or wounded.

The captain asked if I would lead a reaction element to effect a rescue. I pulled a seven-man team together and headed into the bush with little more than adrenaline to cover the three clicks to the ambush site.

Charlie had set up a hasty "horseshoe ambush," so named for its shape. We made a lot of noise as we approached the ambush site. Our hope was to fool the VC into believing we were a larger force than we were. Charlie opened up the horseshoe and let us in. They closed it quickly and opened fire again. I heard Doc yelling and found him under the bamboo bush.

He had two terrible wounds caused by an AK-47 round through the thigh of each leg. Both femurs were completely shattered with sharp bones protruding. He had applied assault packs to each leg as tourniquets which stopped the bleeding. He warned me that to move him without a stretcher would cause him to bleed to death. The sharp bones would slice through his arteries if we weren't careful.

Meanwhile, we were taking fire from three directions. Five hand grenades were thrown onto our position within twenty minutes. Any one or two of them could have finished our entire team. However, an unseen hand was protecting us. The VC had just crossed a deep body of water and all their gear was soaked. As a result, the grenades misfired. When none of their explosives detonated, Charlie evaporated into the bush and we managed to get Doc to safety.

I went back to the ambush site at first light, found the five hand grenades, and detonated them with one of my own. I breathed a sigh of relief as I thought about what might have been. At the time, I couldn't see that God had blessed me with His divine protection. I took credit where credit wasn't mine to take. I bragged about being a marine's marine.

REDEMPTION

I began to wonder as I lay in that attic space. Was I so invulnerable? I had seen death, and had come close enough myself to lose a lot of my arrogance. Though I wasn't quite ready to trust the Lord with my life, I no longer felt so proud and immortal. I wondered if I would live to see my wife again. More days passed, the NVA hadn't come into the room in about twelve hours, and we decided it was time to take a chance. After five days and six nights, we couldn't last much longer.

We entered the house, and the first thing we took was water. We were sick from lack of water and we drank more than we should have. It tasted so good. The occupants came out of their bunker and begged us to leave. If the NVA found us in their house, they would die. We took more water and some small bananas and left.

As we found our way through the city, we were able to rejoin Hotel Company, Second Battalion, Fifth Marines. We learned that the Tet Offensive was still in progress but, by God's providence, we had survived. But I didn't feel like celebrating. The events of those days had caused me to evaluate my life more deeply than I ever had before, but I wasn't quite ready to change. It wasn't until I had returned home and was assigned to debriefing the POWs that my life truly changed.

A number of the POWs came home to "empty" homes. Worse, some came home to learn that their wives had remarried in their absence. God touched my heart deeply as I sat with these men and grieved with them.

I had not wept in years, but I wept for these men as well as for myself. I recognized the emptiness of my life and the waste of living without a higher purpose. As men agonized over the loss of their wives and girlfriends, God began to speak to my heart. My wife, Lenora, was more than I deserved. She was a fine woman, and we had three wonderful children.

She had been praying for me and had been faithful to me. I had been away in Vietnam, but her love and prayers had never left my side. Yet I had never been grateful for that—even through all the close calls I had been through. But now, sitting with men who had lost years of freedom as well as their loved ones, I saw for the first time the emptiness of my life. I saw the emptiness of my heart. I had never been thankful, and now God showed me how much He had done for me. I saw the price He paid for me. It was then that God humbled me and I received Christ as my Savior. Thank the Lord for my dear wife showing me the way to salvation.

A lot of people look at their lives and believe God could never forgive them. Do you want to know how great God's grace is? Look at my life and see His grace.

When I didn't know God, when I didn't want God, when I thought I didn't need God, He was still watching over me. I thought I was a smart man, but I had no answers for the POWs who had lost their families. I thought I was a strong man. But God showed me in Vietnam that no man is strong enough to save himself.

I am so grateful He did.

A TIME
FOR WAR

War is not so heavy a burden as slavery.
Vaugenargues

The last argument of kings.
Latin Saying

And blood in torrents pour
In vain—always in vain,
For war breeds war again.
John Davidson

Every gun that is fired, every warship
launched, every rocket fired signifies,
in the final sense, a theft from those who
hunger and are not fed, those who are cold
and are not clothed.
Dwight D. Eisenhower

HIS SOVEREIGNTY
IN THE STORM

★

SGT. DANIEL B. OLSON
US ARMY

For my thoughts are not your thoughts, Neither are your ways my ways," declares the Lord (Isa. 55:8, NASB).

"Mount up! We're moving out . . . now!"

The word came just as I settled down to get some rest after a sleepless night and nonstop morning. We had two hours to pack up and move out of the Saudi Arabian desert. We had anticipated this order since the start of the air war forty days earlier. By now we were ready to go home. And we knew that for us, the road home led through Iraq.

I was part of the intelligence unit of the Twenty-fourth Mechanized Infantry Division. Our mission was to seize the Iraqi airbase at Jalibah and trap the Iraqi army, preventing their escape from Kuwait. The attack into Iraq wasn't supposed to start until the next day, but the collapse of the Iraqi defenses east of us caused us to move out fifteen hours earlier. I would start the march into Iraq after more than twenty-four hours without sleep.

While army and marine divisions to our east slogged through artillery fire and landmines, our division raced across the empty desert expanse. After thirty hours of non-stop driving, our company finally paused for a six-hour rest. I was physically exhausted. Having been on the go for two days straight, the adrenaline rush had run out. A chilling wind blew sand into my face as I spread my sleeping bag over the rocky landscape and plopped down.

Drops of cold rain on my face interrupted my relief. I looked up at the dark sky in despair as the drops began to intensify. There was no time to erect a tent, and the fierce wind was blowing the rain into every possible refuge.

"God, please, stop this rain!" I cried out in anger and frustration. I begged God to see the depth of my faith. To show Him how much I believed He could stop the rain, I thanked Him for the miracle that would soon come.

And then it happened. The rain came down in sheets!

"Why are you doing this, God?" I pleaded. "Your own Son said that a mustard seed of faith could move a mountain. I only asked that You would move a dark rain cloud!" I was disillusioned that God, who controls the wind and the rain, would not say "Peace! Be still!" After all, I was His child, wet and cold on the desert floor. It was then that I felt the Lord speak to my heart. "Dan, you say you have enough faith to believe that I can stop the rain. Do you have enough faith to trust Me when I say that the rain is for your own good?"

My answer was simple: "No." How could this exhaustion be for my own good? What I needed was rest.

I never did sleep, and the rain continued throughout the night. I lay awake, frustrated and cold until the sunrise, when we mounted up again. We continued the march through the next evening. When we stopped, I collapsed onto my sleeping bag. The rain had stopped and blissful sleep came upon me.

We seized Jalibah after a fierce fight. When the shooting stopped and the smoke cleared, I got a closer look at the destructiveness of the forty-four-day war. I crawled through the bunkers and foxholes abandoned by the enemy, and inspected the area where the Iraqi troops slept the day before. I felt the blankets that the enemy slept under the night it rained so hard. And in that instant God opened my eyes!

The blankets were wet. The holes in the ground were filled with mud. The bunkers stank with mildew.

Could it be that the same rain that kept me awake had demoralized these troops? Did the clouds and blowing sand that made me so miserable conceal our forces as we maneuvered for our attack? Didn't the pouring rain uncover buried Iraqi minefields? And, didn't the stormy weather keep the enemy from using its chemical weapons?

Did the God whose hands control the winds and rain know what was best for me that night as I cried out in desperation?

I humbly bowed my heart and soul at that moment and declared, "He did."

(Used by permission of Command magazine, published by Officers' Christian Fellowship, Englewood, Colorado.)

AIR RAID OVER ISRAEL
(PART 1)

★

You shall not be afraid of the terror by night,
Nor of the arrow that flies by day (Ps. 91:5).

My dad used to tell me, you don't really know what a person will do until the battle begins. He'd served twenty-plus years and had seen his share of battle. He'd seen his share of cowards and heroes. His conclusion was that until someone had his life on the line, you really didn't know his heart. I found out just how true that was during the Gulf War.

Working the line between Syria and Israel, peacekeepers patrolled the no-man zone between the two enemies. It wasn't bad duty, actually. It was a beautiful country with many pleasant sights and diversions. Every peacekeeper had a primary duty and at least one additional duty. The primary duty was obvious—keep the peace, patrol the region, and show the UN flag. My additional duty was to be the assistant evacuation officer in Northern Israel. In the event war began, I was to evacuate civilians. I read the book on evacuation duties and quickly shoved it back in the drawer to collect dust. A thousand captains before me had seen the same book and done the same thing, I reasoned. On with more important matters.

From the small country of Israel, we watched the escalation in Iraq with concern. However, we weren't sure there was going to be a war. In January, 1991, we began to prepare for the worst. I had prepared for the worst hundreds of times before in other circumstances. That didn't mean I expected to have to perform all the things I'd prepared for. Being prepared and facing the *real* thing were totally different concepts. At least they were in *my* mind.

So as the days of January ticked by, many of the nations called their peacekeepers to tell them to send their families home. My family was there at my own expense—what we called "non-command sponsored." Consequently, we had to make a decision. If I sent my wife and children home, we paid for the tickets. More importantly, we had no home in the US anymore. All our goods were in storage. However, my wife wanted our family to stay together unless we were absolutely forced to separate. She was a military wife, and a trooper in every respect. So, along with millions of Israelis, she prepared a "safe room" in our apartment in Tiberias.

We stocked the room with water, batteries, radios, food, blankets, and extra "everything" we could think of. We were given chemical warfare gas masks and trained to use them. Since our youngest was a baby, we were given a small bed covered with a plastic tent for his protection. We placed heavy, plastic fiber tape over the windows of our apartment. If we were bombed, we hoped the tape would keep the windows from shattering into the room. We were ready for whatever came—at least that's what we thought.

On a Monday, the last international airliner flew out of Ben Gurion airport. Things had gotten progressively worse, and Iraq had threatened to bomb Israel. No one but El Al Airlines was willing to risk flying into a potential war zone. We had sealed our fate and now waited for whatever would come.

Tuesday morning, the very next day, I got a call from Jerusalem telling me my family had received orders from Washington. They had been declared "command sponsored." The good news in these orders was that my family's travel costs would be covered when they returned to the United States. The bad news was that they were ordered to evacuate within twenty-four hours. We certainly were not prepared for that.

Half in shock and half in disbelief, we began to pack two suitcases for each of our children and my wife. A Swiss Air prop jet was being flown into Jerusalem airport and then to Cyprus. My wife and children and one other family would be given tickets back to the US at the embassy in Cyprus. But a thousand questions remained. Where would my wife and children go?

The next morning, I packed up the family in the jeep and headed south to Jerusalem. God would have to go with them, because I could not. They faced many uncertainties ahead, but my path seemed clouded as well.

Hundreds of diplomatic personnel needed help to evacuate the country. The station chief had been away on leave. My boss had left as well to accompany his family home. As a senior captain, I had been overseeing the evacuation of a thousand civilians. With time running out, there were many still to care for. Some nationalities were allowed to travel to Damascus and then fly home. Others were not, and we worked diplomatic clearance for them to travel across the Sinai to Cairo Airport. Others caught a ferry from Haifa to Cyprus and then home. All in all, it was very complicated. *I should have been thinking about my own family instead of worrying about all these other things,* I thought. But it was too late. The plane was waiting and anxious to depart. We quickly prayed together as a family, and then they were gone.

I can't describe the empty feeling in the pit of my stomach as I opened the door of our apartment and looked around the empty rooms. I felt my throat tighten as I saw the baby toys scattered on the floor. In room after room, I found reminders of my family. I steeled myself against those feelings and went back to work.

A thousand details waited for me. Leases had to be terminated, goods disposed of, and arrangements made with neighboring countries for exit visas. The next forty-eight hours passed as a blur of frenzied activity. From time to time, I wondered what had happened to my family. Wednesday night, I fell into bed for the first time in almost two days. I awoke the next morning at 9:00 A.M.

As I walked into the UN headquarters in Tiberias, I thought things seemed a bit strange. Peacekeepers were walking around in chemical warfare suits and battle fatigues. I looked at them as strangely as they looked at me.

"What's going on?" I asked.

"Where have you been? We were bombed last night!"

"What? When?"

"Here in northern Israel. Iraq launched SCUDS at us, and the Americans are bombing Iraq!"

I was stunned. "Didn't you hear the sirens?" they asked incredulously.

No, I hadn't heard the sirens. I had been too exhausted to hear anything. I had slept through the first night of the war.

EVACUATION TO UNCERTAINTY (PART 2)

★

CINDY O'LEARY
USAF WIFE

You are my hiding place; You shall preserve me from trouble;
You shall surround me with songs of deliverance.
I will instruct you and teach you in the way you should go;
I will guide you with My eye (Ps. 32:7-8).

A lot of folks would have said, "I told you so. You had no business going over to such a dangerous place with four children." I have always ascribed, however, to the saying of Ruth, who told her mother-in-law, "Where you go, I will go also." I believed that if a daughter-in-law could show such devotion to her mother-in-law, then how much more a wife. So where my husband went, unless we were forbidden, I followed.

Sitting on the plane looking out at the Mediterranean, though, gave me pause to wonder at the wisdom of my situation. As Jerusalem became a speck in the distance, it was hard to keep the tears from forming. I had no idea when, or if, I'd ever see my husband again. In a short time we'd land in Cyprus to make arrangements to return home. Home. . . . Home was in Tiberias, Israel, where we had just left. We had no home in America. I forced myself to push the tears back.

The three older children were unusually subdued. Only baby Sean was his usual rambunctious self. Another military wife and her children accompanied me. It was comforting to have another woman with me who spoke English and shared the pain of the moment. Though we had just met, we quickly became friends. Trouble has a way of bringing strangers close together.

It was after midnight when we finally landed in Cyprus. The taxis were small and we had to hire three of them to get our luggage and us to the hotel. The only rooms available on the island were at the Hyatt and cost $250 a night! For my family of five, I had to rent two rooms.

Though the price was outrageous, I would have managed by putting it on a credit card. The only problem was, I didn't have one. Shortly before being evacuated, my purse had been stolen. We had been forced to cancel our credit cards, and the only identification I had left was my passport. Even my military I.D. was gone. I had no husband to see me through this and make the decisions he'd normally make. I was alone with four children in a foreign country. "God, I need Your help *now*," I prayed fervently. "I have no one else."

In spite of all the uncertainty ahead I was exhausted and slept soundly that night. The next morning I gave instructions to my teens and left one-year-old Sean in their hands. I headed off to face whatever fate awaited me at the American embassy.

The trip to the embassy crossed a border that separated the island between Greece and Turkey. Once on the other side we were greeted by the American attaché, who turned out to be more than we could have hoped for. He was wonderful in every respect. He treated us with great kindness and told us we'd be given tickets to wherever we wanted to go. I thought Hawaii sounded pretty good, but wisely chose to return from where we had begun our Middle East adventure—Omaha, Nebraska.

Our car was stored there, and I'd need it for whatever came next. Then it dawned on me that I'd need a driver's license, a military I.D. card, and about a dozen other things as well. My head hurt until, like Scarlett O'Hara, I decided, "I can't think about that today. I'll worry about that tomorrow."

While tickets were arranged, we were treated to lunch. In the middle of our meal, the attaché answered my most pressing need as he casually asked, "Now, how much money would you like me to advance you to see you through the next week?" God had met my need with abundance. Sometime later that afternoon, we made the trip back across the no-man's land between Greece and Turkey, and

I was reunited with the children. They had survived the torment of changing diapers all day and were thrilled to see me again.

About 2:00 the next morning we were in the airport waiting to board a plane for the US. The stores were closed, but the manager of one shop opened his door so we could listen to the radio. As he turned it on, the English station blared the news, "Baghdad has been bombed!" I stood in stunned silence as I took in this news. It shouldn't have surprised me because Uncle Sam doesn't evacuate citizens without a pretty good reason. Even so, hearing the news brought a heaviness to our hearts.

The trip home to the States was long, involving stops in London and New York. The mood of these airports was somber and security guards were in abundance. All luggage coming out of the Middle East was being checked thoroughly. Finally, we were on the last leg of the journey. After almost a full day in the air, I was ready to get off the plane.

"Will passenger Cindy O'Leary please report to the cockpit," I heard a male voice say over the airplane intercom. My heart froze and I thought, *This can only be bad news.* I was pretty sure they were going to tell me Israel had been bombed and my husband was dead. The captain looked at me and handed me a note. It said, "Your party will meet you on the other side of the gate." My heart rejoiced! Not only was my husband alive, but God had sent someone to meet us.

As I came out of the concourse I saw my husband's close friend waiting for us. He took us to his home and for several days took care of our every need. God had been so good to us. When we were in the fire, He stood beside us. When we were afraid, He comforted us. We still had a long way still to go, but I knew in my heart He would be there to see us through.

D-DAY: TRIAL BY FIRE

★

CHERYL BOSTROM

"Good luck! And let us all beseech the blessing of Almighty God upon this great and noble undertaking."
General Dwight D. Eisenhower, 4 June 1944

"Put on another hundred," shouted the commander. As fast as they could be counted, 9,200 men boarded the warship *Aquitania*—capacity 6,500. German submarines tailed them as they sailed from America to England and finally to the shores of France.

Gray with seasickness, Loren Weldon and other members of his shore party changed from their navy uniforms into army fatigues. They wanted to be sure their fellow Americans could easily recognize them once they landed on the enemy-held shores. As they boarded their landing craft, many reflected on the staggering defenses that lay before them. Many pondered the chaplain's words spoken moments before. Loren prayed for His God to be close to Him and those with him.

The ramps of their landing craft opened onto the stormy shores of Omaha Beach in southern France. Loren and thirty other men of the Sixth Naval Beach Battalion waded through sandbars and debris to help crack the Atlantic Wall. Loren was stunned by the carnage from air strikes and earlier assault waves that morning.

Demolished vehicles as well as dead and wounded soldiers were strewn everywhere. "We could hardly get onto the beach," Loren reflected. "The men were fearful and trembling."

Unfortunately, some of the soldiers in the first assaults had worn their small flotation tubes too low on their waist. When they inflated their tubes, the men were flipped upside down. The weight in their packs and ammunition left them helpless, and they drowned.

"I wasn't afraid to die, because I knew God." Loren's unshakable faith kept him from the sheer panic that surrounded him. Once on shore he immediately began digging a hole to climb into for protection. The tide would be coming in, and he knew he couldn't stay there long. He risked the withering gunfire, moved further up the beach, and began to dig again.

"Don't dig! Don't dig!" shouted one soldier. As he looked beneath his hands, he saw the metal covering of a land mine. He began to move carefully away from the container of death beneath his hands. An hour later German airplanes began to strafe the beach, blasting it with firepower that left them shocked and stunned.

"Our troops were so scattered and fragmented," Loren said with a lump in his throat. "Shrapnel was piercing right through our helmets."

Night fell, and then at first light, Loren began to scan the beach for other members of his company. Looking up and down the beach, he saw two more boats as they landed. Immediately, artillery found and obliterated them. An ammunition barge arrived next and exploded moments later in a fireworks of noise and sound. The muffled clatter of exploding ammunition continued throughout that day and into the next.

Loren managed to survive that day to continue working on Omaha Beach for the next six weeks. Relaying messages, carrying the wounded, and delivering supplies turned into a moment-by-moment struggle for life.

"The rancid smell of the dead is something I will never forget." Loren urged all that would listen, "Stay close to the Lord in prayer and thank Him for every day. He wants us to rest our souls in Him. He is a great God!"

Certainly, God provided a great deliverance on that great and terrible day.

This is the recollection of one veteran, now ninety-two years old, of June 6, 1944. (World WarII veterans are now dying at the rate of approximately one thousand per day. Just before this story went to print, Loren went home to be with the Lord. Shortly before he died,

Loren said, "I'm ready for my robe of righteousness." Another saint has run his race and received his "Well done, thou good and faithful servant!")

(Used by permission of Command magazine, published by Officers' Christian Fellowship, Englewood, Colorado.)

A SIGN FOR HIS PEOPLE

★

DONNA ADAMS
USMC WIFE

Be strong and of good courage, do not fear nor be afraid of them;
for the Lord your God, He is the One who goes with you.
He will not leave you nor forsake you (Deut. 31:6)

Early in 1991, my husband, then-Lieutenant Jake Adams, spent his time surveying the flat, endless desert spaces of Saudi Arabia. Jake's artillery battalion (Second Battalion, Twelfth Marines) was part of Operation Desert Storm designed to liberate Kuwait. As they traveled through this country, they often observed smoke that moved across the sky from oil fires, driven by the west-to-east prevailing winds.

Shortly before the ground war began, he took a picture of the oil fires burning on the horizon along the border of Saudi Arabia and Kuwait. In late February, anxiety among the marines in Jake's unit intensified. Captain Lusk, a naval intelligence officer, called a meeting to brief them about the situation their unit would face during the coming attack.

As he referred to a large map of the desert, he told them that the danger of their situation was clear and imminent. His information was specific: a brigade of Iraqi tanks was positioned a little over two kilometers from where the marines would be attacking. Later that day, Jake learned that Second Battalion, Twelfth Marines would initially provide the general fire support. This support would provide cover for the entire Second Marine Division, but it would place his unit in a very exposed and dangerous position.

The commander of Bravo Battery asked Jake, as the Protestant lay-leader, to assemble the marines for a prayer service on Sunday. It was two hours prior to the advance party scheduled to move toward Kuwait.

Jake spoke to the marines about the courage of Joshua and Caleb during their mission as spies in the Promised Land. He used the example of their fearlessness to encourage the marines for the coming battle. This story seemed appropriate in light of the estimate of ten thousand allied casualties to evict Iraq from Kuwait. Most of them would occur on the ground. Jake then prayed and asked for God's protecting hand to be upon the marines. The service ended and the call to advance was given.

As the troops began their advance that afternoon, the prevailing winds surprisingly shifted 180 degrees. With this change in wind direction, a large black cloud moved quickly into view. It extended from horizon to horizon. Within thirty minutes, as he snapped pictures, the cloud turned the sky to total darkness. Jake couldn't see his hand in front of his face.

Although it was black as ink, Jake and the other marines continued to advance, driving their Humvees, transporting personnel and equipment. With virtually no visibility, it took significantly longer to reach their first fighting position. As they arrived, the recent rains had created wet, cold conditions. Next to them was the reported position of an Iraqi tank brigade.

As they settled into their positions that night they knew just two clicks away was an Iraqi tank brigade. Jake knew the morning would mean either his unit or the Iraqi unit would perish. He slept fitfully until just before the morning light crept across the desert sand.

His men stood at their artillery positions, poised to launch their fusillade when the "fire" command was given. The command came as expected and the ground war of Desert Storm began.

Jake's unit began to fire several hundred rounds on Iraqi positions. They fired and fired and then they waited. They waited for the inevitable advance of Iraqi tanks against their position. But when the sun rose high on the cloudy, smoke-filled horizon, the marines found the landscape—empty! No tanks were in sight. Surprised and relieved, the Second Battalion, Twelfth Marines held their position while the Second Marine Division continued attacking into Kuwait City. Jack and his unit had survived that day. They survived a very dangerous situation without a single casualty, and Jake was thankful for God's protecting hand.

While waiting to return home from Desert Storm, Jake received a letter from our pastor in Oahu, Hawaii. The pastor wrote that the people of Hope Chapel had been praying for Jake. The comfort of knowing this led him to reflect on the unusual black cloud that had hidden the marines during their movement, greatly reducing their vulnerability to counterattack. He realized that the cloud had much more significance after the Lord brought this Bible passage to his heart.

And the Angel of God, who went before the camp of Israel, moved and went behind them; and the pillar of cloud went from before them and stood behind them. So it came between the camp of the Egyptians and the camp of Israel. Thus it was a cloud and darkness to the one, and it gave light by night to the other, so that the one did not come near the other all that night (Ex. 14:19-20).

Just as God protected the Hebrew people from the Egyptians in Moses' time, so He protected my husband and the Second Marine Division during their time of need. I learned by experience that even the clouds obey their Maker.

(Used by permission of Command magazine, published by Officers' Christian Fellowship, Englewood, Colorado.)

A TIME
TO FORGIVE

It is in pardoning that we are pardoned.
St. Francis of Assisi

We forgive to the extent we love.
Duc François La Rochefoucauld

*I think if God forgives us we must forgive
ourselves. Otherwise it is almost like set-
ting up ourselves as a higher tribunal
than Him.*
C.S. Lewis

A LIGHT IN THE DARKNESS

★

FATHER ABBIT
POW 1941-1943

Praise ye the Lord. Praise the Lord, O my soul.
While I live will I praise the Lord: I will sing praises unto my God
while I have any being (Ps. 146:1-2, KJV).

As the new century begins, my experience in the early 1940s seems long ago indeed. War has a way of coming upon you without warning, and the consequences are terrible. These consequences are not only for those who actively participate, but also gravely affect those caught in the crossfire. It seems to disproportionately afflict the innocent—those who have no interest, involvement, or arguments with those at war. I'd have to say I was put in such a situation during the early days of World War II.

I'd been serving a very primitive people as a missionary priest on the southern island of Mindanao in 1941 to establish and sustain an agricultural school that would benefit the very poor on that small island.

It was then that the Japanese bombed Pearl Harbor and the Philippines one early December morning. In the general confusion that followed the declaration of war, people rushed from village to village seeking a safe haven.

We heard terrible stories about what the Japanese soldiers were doing and how they treated their enemies and innocent women. Taking the advice of the United States Army, we resettled in Northern Mindanao. The army believed this would be the safest place. Yet, soon after settling there, we were stunned to learn that General Wainwright was going to surrender to the Japanese. As civilians, we were advised to do the same. By then it was May, 1942, and we were truly terrified.

It never occurred to me that God's plan for my life would result in my being imprisoned. Yet, that is what happened as the Japanese seized the island. I became their prisoner for the next three years.

I was taken captive along with 250 other American and British citizens. The city of Dovaou, along the southern coast of Mindanao, became a prisoner of war concentration camp. It's hard to imagine, but we were taken to a former Philippine night club, called (of all names) The Happy Life Blues. This building, just outside the city of Dovaou, served as our place of internment. We were kept there for more than eighteen months until December of 1943.

While imprisoned, we were forced to endure many inhuman indignities. Degradation and base humiliation, along with starvation, were our constant companions. There are many stories I could tell of those years. Yet, one event that occurred near Christmas stands out most vividly.

It was 1943 and just two days before Christmas. We had suffered a lot and thought we'd received an early Christmas gift when the guards told us we were going to be moved. It seems the Japanese commander decided we would be relocated to the Santa Thomas prison camp in Manila. A few of us were jubilant, little realizing that we were being taken to a starvation camp already housing over four thousand prisoners. Our joy turned to desolation.

On Christmas Eve we were put in the hold of a Japanese troop ship. We were told we would be kept there for ten days during the journey to Manila. It was winter, the cargo hold was black, and we were packed together. Before our guards closed the hatch to the cargo hold, they left us with this news, "Since there are American submarines in these waters, you will probably be torpedoed." And with that, they slammed the hatch closed and locked it with a resounding clap.

It was black inside that floating tomb and we felt the blackness of despair creep into our hearts. We were left with our own thoughts and fears. Labored breathing and one or two muffled sobs were the only sounds we heard. The message that seemed to come from that dark, wet coffin was that we were alone and forsaken.

Then, ever so softly, out of the bleakness and blackness of the night, a lady's beautiful voice began to sing. Softly and timidly, she sang, "Silent Night, Holy Night." The breathing around me became less labored. The sobs ceased. All listened to the sweet, soft voice, and our eyes filled with tears. Our hearts filled with a quiet hope. As she continued her sweet song of praise, all of us, one by one, joined our voices to hers.

We sang of the wonder of Christ's birth from full hearts in desperate circumstances. That night we offered our thoughts and prayers to the Christ Child. We praised Him, not from the padded pews of a stained glass cathedral, but from the black hole of a Japanese troop ship. As we sang, the terror we felt inside fled from us. It could no longer remain there because the presence of Christ had come—just as He had come on Christmas, 2,000 years before.

FORGIVE YOUR ENEMIES

★

But I say to you, love your enemies, bless those who curse you,
do good to those who hate you, and pray for those who spitefully
use you and persecute you, that you may be sons of your Father in
heaven; for He makes His sun rise on the evil and on the good, and
sends rain on the just and on the unjust (Matt. 5: 44-45a).

While serving as a peacekeeper in the Sinai Peninsula, I spent a lot of time in a Jeep patrolling vast quantities of sand. Numerous Bedouins lived in this region; their nomadic lifestyle meant populations as well as sand shifted with the winds.

Part of our aim in the UN was to spread goodwill wherever and whenever possible. In this region, it was the custom of the desert to share tea with those passing by. So I stopped at a Bedouin camp I passed one late summer afternoon.

I was greeted warmly and escorted into a large tent where I was served a glass of hot tea by one of the men. I carefully held the hot glass between my thumb and first finger to keep it from burning my hand. My calluses weren't as thick as my hosts', and the heat on my fingers kept my attention. My host surprised me by speaking fairly comprehensible English, which I appreciated since my Arabic was quite limited.

As we neared the end of our tea, our conversation took an interesting turn. My host looked at another Bedouin across the camp, pointed at him, and said, "Do you see that man over there tending the camels?"

I looked and said, "Yes."

"He's a camel thief," he said with disgust in his voice.

I was surprised and said so. "Why do you have a camel thief tending your camels?"

He ignored my question and said, "He comes from a long line of camel thieves. His father was a camel thief, his grandfather—they're all camel thieves. In fact, he's stolen *my* family's camels."

I thought about this for a while, confused. "Well, if he stole your camels, why don't you just go get them back?"

He replied with less volume, "Well, it happened a long time ago."

I thought about that for a little while longer. Now I was really confused. Another question and I'd be on dangerous ground. My mind danced between diplomacy or satisfying my curiosity. Curiosity won out.

"How long ago?" I asked carefully.

My host spit out, "Eight hundred years, but he's still a camel thief and so is his entire family." And with that, he got up and stormed across the camp. I watched him trail away in the dust and looked at the other men sitting in the circle. They avoided my eyes. I took this to mean our conversation and tea time had ended.

As I mounted my Jeep, I was struck by the realization that peace would be a long time coming to the Middle East. If such hatred was harbored within one Bedouin tribe, how much more between Arab and Jew?

I always had believed forgiveness was meant for the person who wronged me. And, to a certain extent I'm sure that's true. Much more than that, this incident taught me that forgiveness is for me, to release my heart from the bitterness that would twist and destroy it. Forgiveness is not just a gift we give; it is a gift we receive.

SOVIET UNION
SHOOT-DOWN

★

LT. COL. MARK SIMPSON
USAF

The one who loves his brother abides in the light and
there is no cause for stumbling in him. But the one who hates
his brother is in the darkness and walks in the darkness, and
does not know where he is going because the darkness has
blinded his eyes (1 John 2:10-11, NASB).

On September 2, 1958 an allied intelligence listening post recorded the following transmission between Soviet air defense ground controllers and a flight of four MIG-17 interceptor pilots as they shot down an Air Force C-130 reconnaissance aircraft over Soviet Armenia:

582 *"I see the target; a large one. Its altitude is 100 [10,000 meters]*
      as you said."

201 *"I am attacking the target."*

201 *"218 . . . Attack! Attack! The target is a transport; four engine."*

582 *"The target is burning."*

201 *"218 . . . Are you attacking?"*

218 *"Yes . . . I . . . [unintelligible] . . . The tail assembly is falling off*
      the target . . ."

201 *"Look at him; I will finish him off, boys; I will finish him of*
      f on the run. . . . The target has lost control; it's going down."
End of transmission

Though I was only three months old at the time, this transmission was to have the most profound effect upon my life.

Ask people what they remember of the Cold War, and you will get a wide variety of answers. For many, Cold War memories revolve around the air raid drills of the late 1950s and early 1960s, around Gary Francis Powers, or around the Cuban Missile Crisis.

A younger generation may remember the Cold War only by the crumbling of the Berlin Wall. Unknown to many Americans, the Cold War was fought globally on many fronts. Many American military personnel paid the ultimate sacrifice for global peace. US crews manned nuclear components of the strategic triad while others stood at the ready with tactical weapon systems deployed around the world.

During the Cold War, a relatively small group of aviators made up of flight crews and airborne reconnaissance operators gathered information for the National Security Agency's Central Security Service. Eighteen types of air force and navy aircraft were shot down during the Cold War. Information on these missions, shrouded for decades in secrecy, was recently declassified.

As a young child in the 60s, the Cold War meant hiding under my desk at school. Later, as an air force navigator, I fought the Cold War sitting nuclear alert in both the B-52 and B-1 bombers.

But most importantly for me, the Cold War had a darker meaning.

My father, Captain John E. Simpson, was a pilot who flew highly sensitive reconnaissance missions along the borders of the Soviet Union in the late 1950s. A few C-130As, widely known for their tactical aircraft role, were refitted to perform airborne signal reconnaissance. On September 2, 1958 one of these 130s flying the border of Turkey and Soviet Armenia was shot down after being attacked by a flight of four MIG-17s. The entire crew of seventeen—six flight deck personnel and eleven reconnaissance operators—was lost. One of those was my father.

My mother was left in her mid-twenties with two boys—John Jr. (four years old) and me (three months). She knew nothing more than that her husband had died in a crash on a rocky hillside inside the Soviet Union. Later that fall, the family received word that negotiations between the two superpowers had resulted in six sets of remains being repatriated to the United States; four sets were positively identified. My father's remains were one of the four returned to their families in late 1958. The other two bodies were interred in Arlington National Cemetery in "Unknown" graves.

Growing up, I developed a deep-seated hatred for the Russians — hatred fueled by world events and by family members. The hatred and bitterness that came from not knowing my father resulted in my adopting a rather rebellious lifestyle.

But God was at work, even though I didn't know it. I became a Christian during high school, though God still had a lot of work to do in my heart.

I left home for college and joined the Air Force ROTC. Upon joining, I was asked whether I had any reservations about delivering nuclear weapons. I responded coldly, "Not in the least. Where do I sign?" My initial military goals were to "nuke" the communists and to get the real story about my father.

I entered active duty in 1982 and began to hone my aeronautical skills. In the Strategic Air Command, I became one of the most accurate and deadly bombardiers in the force. My family had put my father on a pedestal. I made him into a god and was trying to worship him the best way I could.

Bitterness-induced darkness enveloped my life despite my Christian beliefs. I sought the world and my earthly father, and that blinded me spiritually for the first eight years of my air force career. As relations thawed between the US and Soviet Union, I was surprised and confused. The Cold War had been won, but my personal cold war was unresolved.

In 1993, the two superpowers began to exchange information on aircraft shot down during the previous fifty years. Russia finally admitted to shooting down the RC-130 my dad was piloting. As documents were declassified, the cold war in my heart began to thaw.

The final chapter in the battle for my heart took place a year later. I was given the opportunity to share my story at a Bible study at Air Combat Command Headquarters. That day three former Soviet officers sat in front of me. The Holy Spirit moved in my heart as I spoke. As I finished, I turned to those former enemies and asked them to forgive me for hating them and their people for so many years.

A broken spirit coupled with forgiveness opened the doors to healing, not only for me but also, perhaps, for those ambassadors from Eastern Europe.

Several years later, I was reunited with the other war orphans who lost their fathers on that terrible day in 1958. We stood with families and friends as a memorial to their service was unveiled in Fort Meade, Maryland. The following day, my father was again remembered at Arlington National Cemetery. As the bugler sounded taps and guns sounded their final salute, we were able to close the door on this chapter of our lives.

As I drove away from the cemetery, tears, which had been choked back in the past, ran down my face. My eyes swept past the thousands of white headstones that stood in silent tribute to fallen compatriots. The Spirit reminded me that the living weren't there. My father was alive in heaven, and in that I took great comfort.

I rejoiced to feel alive again. The spirit of a heavy heart had been lifted and replaced with an unsurpassable peace. Jesus had fought and won my personal cold war. It was finished when I loosened my grip on the sword of bitterness and laid it at my Savior's feet.

(Used by permission of Command magazine, published by Officers' Christian Fellowship, Englewood, Colorado.)

OLD VET AT DEATH'S DOOR

★

Say to them: "As I live," says the Lord God, "I have no pleasure in
the death of the wicked, but that the wicked turn from his way and
live" (Ezek. 33:11).

A lot of folks never really give much thought to God until they're knocking on death's door. I met an old man in such a state to an extreme I had never seen before, and I've seen death several times. As I approached this man's hospital bed, I sensed a very dark and foreboding presence. If there is such a being called "Death," as the Scriptures say, it was there in that room. To explain the events that took place that day, I need to first describe how I came to be there.

While stationed in Montgomery, Alabama, I was an active member in a local church. Julie, one of the women in our Bible study, had been ministering in the local jail and shared a prayer request with the group. "I've been ministering to a girl in the local jail who has become a believer in the past couple of months. She grew up in a terribly abusive household. She was physically and sexually abused and ran away from home. As she rebelled against all authority, she found herself in jail. During this time, she has come to know the Lord and is now praying for her father, Bob,[28] who caused her so much pain. She has asked me to go to her father and tell him she forgives him and God loves him. Not just this, but she wants me to lead him to the Lord."

She went on, "As a woman, I feel very uncomfortable being in the same room with this man. He is very, very sick and dying of colon cancer. Even so, knowing what he has done makes it hard for me to even think of being with him."

I looked at Julie and said, "Cindy and I will go with you this afternoon to pray for him." A visible look of relief came across her face, and that afternoon we drove the thirty miles to the hospital.

Anyone who's been to a veterans hospital knows that they exist on a shoestring. The conditions aren't what most folks would like to see around their sick loved ones. But Bob had no loved ones visiting him. His only child was in the local jail praying for him.

The room was still and the air seemed very heavy. Bob barely filled half the bed. The disease had shrunk his size considerably. He had days of stubble on his face, and his arms were bruised from the IV lines and injections he'd been receiving. Clearly, he was being kept comfortable until the time for his passing.

I held his gray, shriveled hand and felt more bone than skin. "Bob, Bob. Are you there, Bob? I've come to pray for you today. Your daughter asked us to come to you." Bob was not with me in any way. He seemed in a deep sleep or drug-induced coma. I called him again, "Bob, I've come to pray for you. Bob, wake up. Bob, are you there?" Still, I received no response.

Julie said, "We'll just pray for him and then we can go."

But I thought, *This old man is going to die, and probably today. When he leaves here, he'll never know another moment of peace for eternity.* I felt the Spirit of God rise up inside me. I couldn't quit now! "Bob!" I spoke louder and my wife closed the door to the room. I couldn't let this old vet die without hearing at least once that Jesus died for him and that God loved him.

I rubbed his shoulder. I touched his hair and continued to talk to him, trying to rouse him from his sleep. Anyone watching would have thought I'd lost my senses. Twenty minutes later, Bob began to rouse from his sleep. It was another ten minutes before he could look me in the eye. Five minutes after that he spoke his first words. Thirty-five minutes passed before he responded to my voice. I told him how much Jesus loved him and about God's plan of salvation for him.

I began to talk very slowly to him. Stopping often, I'd ask, "Do you understand, Bob?" He'd shake his head affirmatively. Finally, I asked him to pray with me and led him in the prayer of salvation. A smile was on his face for a fleeting minute when we finished, and then he slipped back into unconsciousness. The old vet was at peace, I felt, but still a doubt nagged at me. *Did he really pray with me? Did he receive the Lord in His heart? I guess I'll never know.*

The phone rang a few days later with the news about Bob. No, he wasn't dead. In fact, the old veteran had made an astonishing recovery. His bleeding had stopped, his vital signs stabilized, and he had been released from the hospital. At about the same time, his daughter was released from jail and came home to find her father waiting for her.

She later told us she just about fainted when, for the first time in her life, she heard her father humbly say, "I am so very sorry. Please, please forgive me." The words she had longed to hear now rang in her ears and she hugged him and whispered, "I forgive you, Daddy."

Three weeks later, Bob sat down in his easy chair on the porch. In the afternoon breeze, he went to sleep and never woke up. His daughter found him resting there and wept on his lap. The old vet had fought his last battle. Through the prayers and love of a forgiving daughter, God had won the final victory.

A TIME
FOR LAST WORDS

Therefore we also, since we are surrounded by so great a cloud of witnesses, let us lay aside every weight, and the sin which so easily ensnares us, and let us run with endurance the race that is set before us

(Heb. 12:1).

RUNNING INTO THE SAVIOR'S ARMS

★

Traveling around the world, I have seen poverty that most only see on television. In India I was pierced as I watched orphans struggling to find a bowl of rice a day. What could I possibly do in the face of such dire and widespread circumstances? I was a full-time Air Force officer living on the other side of the world. I turned away, disappointed. But then I sensed God speaking to my heart saying, *"You* can make a difference here."

After returning to the US, I continued to feel this tug at my heart. I couldn't walk away and do nothing. It wasn't enough to *feel* someone's pain when you could ease it. I felt a strong belief I could. So, in a very small way, a friend of mine and I pooled our funds and opened the doors of our first orphanage in India. Jesus fed 5,000 by starting with five loaves and two fish. Could we do the same?

As you might guess, running an orphanage was a lot more expensive and difficult than we expected. We were forced to move out of three buildings through eviction, and two others following cyclones in the first two years. We decided to build our own permanent orphanage facility and opened the doors early in 1992. Since then we have built two other orphanages and are in the process of building a fourth. Additionally we have built over twenty churches and have opened a home for indigent Christian widows.

Today, we have more than 120 children in our full-time care. We have seen children grow up, marry, and have children of their own—new Christian families making an impact in their world. Our support for these children involves shelter, clothing, medical care, food, and schooling as well as Christian education. Additionally, we often help our children into adulthood by paying for technical training or additional education to enable them with life skills.

Finally, we feed thousands of hungry children who have stood at the gates of our facilities. It has been estimated that orphans on the streets in India have a life expectancy of twelve years. For many in the West, it is difficult to imagine that nakedness and hunger continue to stalk so many who are so helpless.

It has also been estimated that there are more than 100,000 orphans on the streets of Bombay alone. As Christians, I believe we must examine how we are running our race for Christ, considering how many lives hang in the balance.

The Lord showed me, "You can make a difference here." To do so, I must run a race unencumbered by simple pleasures that many take for granted. I have a vivid sense of the soon coming day when I cross the finish line. I'm going to run full speed into the arms of Jesus. I don't want to feel disappointed on the day I first look into His face. I want to *know* I gave my all to those He brought to my door. I want to be the kind of person who took the talents God gave him and multiplied them as Christ multiplied the loaves of bread.

We can be the loaves and *we* can be the fish. All that is left for us is to be willing to be used for Him. He is the God who parted the Red Sea, fed the 5,000, and came back from the dead. I believe He can do more than I imagine; he has proven it to me again and again.

Do you have a heart to run a race worthy of the One who called you? The Lord is waiting for such people, "For the eyes of the Lord move to and fro throughout the earth that He may strongly support those whose heart is completely His" (2 Chron. 16: 9 NASB).

The world is also waiting for people who will live lives upon the high ground. Those who believe life is more than power, fame, or money. You don't have to be perfect to live a life on the high ground. You do have to be willing.

If you would join me, then prepare for more difficulty, more heartbreak, more joy, and more excitement than you can ever begin to imagine. It's a journey I must make. It's a journey that will not wait. For those taking the high ground—I look forward to seeing you there! God speed you on your way.

Your fellow servant in Christ,

Jeff O'Leary

Colonel Jeff O'Leary can be reached at www.jeffoleary.com for speaking engagements. Information about Mission of Joy and its work among orphans can be found at www.missionjoy.org.

ENDNOTES AND SOURCES

[1] For more information on this incident see David Barton's *The Bulletproof George Washington*, Aledo, TX: WallBuilder Press, 1990.

[2] Bancroft, George, *Bancroft's History of the United States, Vol IV*, Third Edition, Boston: Charles C. Little & James Brown, 1838, p. 190.

[3] Johnson, William J., *George Washington, the Christian*, Nashville, Tennessee, Abingdon Press, 1919, pp. 41-42.

[4] Banvard, Joseph, *Tragic Scenes in the History of Maryland and the Old French War*, Boston: Gould and Lincoln, 1856, p. 154.

[5] Marshall, Peter and Manuel, David, *The Light and the Glory*, New Jersey: Flemming H. Revell Co., 1977, pp. 312-315. Used with permission.

[6] Name changed

[7] Magee, John Gillespie, Jr., "High Flight." Copyright holder unknown.

[8] Kimball, Bill, The Other Side of Glory. Reprinted with permission.

[9] Name changed

[10] PFC Johnson's actions earned him a posthumous Congressional Medal of Honor.

[11] Name changed.

[12] Commager, Henry Steele, *The Blue and the Gray, pp. 415-416.*

[13] *Christ in the Camp*

[14] Southall, Douglas, *Lee's Lieutenants*, p. 241

[15] Commager, p. 416.

[16] Wiley, Bell Irvin, *The Life of Johnny Reb*, pp. 183-184.

[17] Robertson, James, *Stonewall Jackson*, p 666.

[18] Freeman, Douglas Southall, *Lee's Lieutenants*, p. 244.

[19] Robertson, pp.689-690

[20] Freeman.

[21] Robertson, p. 666.

[22] Roberston, p. 685.

[23] Wiley, p. 181.

[24] Wiley, pp. 176-182.

[25] Henderson, pp. 398-399.

[26] For security reasons, the name has been masked.

[27] Gary Francis Powers was an USAF pilot who was shot down over the Soviet Union in 1960 while flying a U-2. He survived and was later tried as a "spy" by the Soviet Union. He was repatriated a year later in a prisoner exchange.

[28] Name Changed

A Personal Note From the Author

More than just to entertain, Cook Communications Ministries hopes to inspire you to fulfill the great commandments to love God with all your heart, soul, mind, and strength and your neighbor as yourself. Towards that end, the author wishes to share these personal thoughts with you.

HEART:

More than ever, I believe America is in need of models. Not perfect models, for apart from Christ, there is no such thing. Yet, we need examples of those who have decided to choose a different road, a higher road, while facing the same difficult choices we ourselves face each day. The stories within are designed to strengthen you by giving strong examples of military believers who took the high ground when they could have chosen a less noble course. If they encourage you, if they strengthen you or motivate you to a life of greater virtue, then I have accomplished my purpose.

SOUL:

My life has been committed to strengthening the weak, the orphan, and the widow. This Scripture calls me to this labor of love: "With this news, strengthen those who have tired hands, and encourage those who have weak knees. Say to those who are afraid, 'Be strong, and do not fear, for your God is coming . . . He is coming to save you. And when he comes, he will open the eyes of the blind and unstop the ears of the deaf. The lame will leap like a deer, and those who cannot speak will shout and sing!'" (Isa. 35:3-6, NLT).

MIND: I encourage you to draw near to the Lord, listen to His

voice, and obey what He tells you. Growing in Him comes from being nurtured daily by Him. I encourage you to seek opportunities to serve in His name. If you desire to learn more about reaching those in desperate need, please visit our web site at www.jeffoleary.com or www.missionjoy.org. Each day 43,000 children die around the world. We're trying to make a difference in the lives of those the Lord has brought to our door.

STRENGTH: What then shall we do? Strengthen what remains.

Be the model for your world of what Christ calls us to be. The power of one filled with the Spirit of God is beyond our imagination. The only question remaining is: Will you?

My prayer on the next page is that you will awaken to the possibilities before you and make a difference in your world.

I look beneath my feet and see the wasted days, lazy months,
   and empty years,
My life, poured out like water, without purpose into the sand.
I cannot hold on to the water you send; It comes in with the
   dawn and drains away by sunset.
But Lord, before it empties into the sand, direct this
   precious water:
To the thirsty, Lord, quench their parched throats,
To the hungry, Lord, quiet the pangs within,
To the empty, Lord, fill their hungry souls.

Until the day when the water no longer flows through
   my hands,
When you place your wounded hand in mine and
   lead me home,
Use these hands to pour Your water on the
Unquenched, unfilled, and unsatisfied.
Before another sunrise becomes another sunset,
Before this water empties uselessly into the sand, Lord—
Awaken my soul to the wonder of a life poured out
Serving You.

Jeffrey O'Leary